THE

HIP

POCKET GUIDE

TO OFFBEAT

WISDOM

Bill Sauer

BY

WILLIAM SAUER

The Hip Pocket Guide to Offbeat Wisdom

William Sauer

215 Pages
Published by Author
Date Published: 11/2005
ISBN 1-4116-6076-5

Author Info

William Sauer is a corporate communications manager in Rochester, New York. He is passionate about words and ideas, and views life as the ultimate creative challenge. He lives in Rochester with his wife Nancy, daughter Katie and son Jon.

Introduction

"The Hip Pocket Guide to Offbeat Wisdom" has been an obsessive labor of love for me for close to two decades now. That was when I began jotting down passages I happened upon in books that struck me as remarkable, amusing, or useful. As I'm a voracious reader, my collection of jottings expanded quickly. Soon it occurred to me that other people might enjoy these quotations and cultural references, too.

In today's hectic, info-byte world, it seems that there might be tremendous value in a far-ranging anthology of succinct and profound quotations. Short as they are, these pithy entries of thirty words or less strike me as anything but the literary equivalent of fast food. Rather, they inspire the active intellectual engagement all great literature offers, and they invite the reader to drill down into deeper levels of meaning and interpretation. Some of them almost seem self-contradictory – for example, Paul Gauguin's "I shut my eyes in order to see." – yet unfold with the beauty and crystalline clarity of a Zen koan.

The originators of the quotations presented here range from Popeye to Picasso, from Johnny Rotten to Jesus. I've chosen and arranged them very deliberately, doing my best to give them a chance to play off, amplify and inform each other – a feature I hope readers will enjoy, and which is unlike anything offered by any other collection I've seen.

How I've pulled the collection together may or may not reflect my own temperament, with its eastern influenced mysticism, Germanic penchant for deep thought, and slightly off-center sensibility. In any case, I find these collected quotations wonderful in many ways – as intellectual chewing gum, as idea-and-reflection-generators, and as conversational Tabasco®. I hope you'll find them inspirational too, and that reading "The Hip Pocket Guide to Offbeat Wisdom" will be as enjoyable for you as creating it has been for me.

Contents

Action

Never mistake motion for action.
    Ernest Hemingway

The mark of a good action is that it appears inevitable in retrospect.
    Robert Louis Stevenson

Action, to be effective, must be directed to clearly conceived ends.
    Jawaharlal Nehru

All actions are based on intentions.
    Prophet Muhammad

It is not enough to be compassionate. You must act.
    Tenzin Gyatso, 14th Dalai Lama

On action alone be thine interest, Never on its fruits.
    Bhagavadgita

Do what you can, with what you have, where you are.
    Theodore Roosevelt

A man is the sum of his actions, of what he has done, of what he can do,
Nothing else.
    André Malraux

To think is easy. To act is hard. But the hardest thing in the world is to act in
accordance with your thinking.
    Johann Wolfgang von Goethe

I hear and I forget. I see and I remember. I do and I understand.
    Confucius

Action is the only answer to conquer fear.
    Norman Vincent Peale

You miss 100 percent of the shots you never take.
    Wayne Gretzky

Action may not always bring happiness; but there is no happiness without action.
    Benjamin Disraeli

He that has done nothing has known nothing.
    Thomas Carlyle

Even if you are on the right track, you'll get run over if you just sit there.
    Will Rogers

In action, be primitive; in foresight, a strategist.
René Char

The most decisive actions of our life – I mean those that are most likely to decide the whole course of our future – are, more often than not, unconsidered.
André Gide

Inaction may be the highest form of action.
Jerry Brown

Action: the last recourse of those who know not how to dream.
Oscar Wilde

Act quickly, think slowly.
Greek Proverb

The test of any man lies in action.
Pindar

Well done is better than well said.
Benjamin Franklin

Give me the ready hand rather than the ready tongue.
Giuseppe Garibaldi

Actions speak louder than words.
Proverb

An ounce of action is worth a ton of theory.
Friedrich Engels

Action will remove the doubts that theory cannot solve.
Tehyi Hsieh

I have always thought the actions of men the best interpreters of their thoughts.
John Locke

Action is the antidote to despair.
Joan Baez

This is a world of action, and not for moping and droning in.
Charles Dickens

A thought which does not result in an action is nothing much, and an action which does not proceed from a thought is nothing at all.
Georges Bernanos

The ancestor of every action is a thought.
Ralph Waldo Emerson

The great end of life is not knowledge but action.
Thomas Henry Huxley

The wise see knowledge and action as one; they see truly.
Bhagavad Gita

Adversity

Every calamity is a spur and valuable hint.
Ralph Waldo Emerson

There is no education like adversity.
Benjamin Disraeli

Adversity is the first path to Truth.
Lord Byron

Adversity introduces a man to himself.
Anonymous

The man who has no problems is out of the game.
Elbert G. Hubbard

Where there is no strife there is decay: "the mixture which is not
shaken decomposes."
Heraclitus

All things are difficult before they are easy.
John Norley

God gives almonds to those who have no teeth.
Spanish Proverb

To thicken the plot.
The Indian Saint Ramakrishna, when asked why there is evil in the world

He knows not his own strength that hath not met adversity.
Ben Jonson

Adversity has the effect of eliciting talents, which in prosperous circumstances
would have lain dormant.
Horace

Tragedy wonderfully reveals the nature of man.
        John Kenneth Galbraith

Fire is the test of gold; adversity of strong men.
        Seneca

That which does not kill me makes me stronger.
        Fredrich Nietzsche

Illegitimis non carborundum.
Pseudo-Latin, Don't let the bastards grind you down.
        General Joseph Stilwell

We are confronted with insurmountable opportunities.
        Walt Kelly

No plan survives contact with the enemy.
        Field Marshall Helmuth Carl Bernard von Moltke

Adversity reveals genius, prosperity conceals it.
        Horace

It's not the load that breaks you down, it's the way you carry it.
        Lena Horne

Smooth seas do not make skillful sailors.
        African Proverb

Afterlife

Now I go to seek a great perhaps.
        Francois Rabelais, attributed remark on his deathbed

I do not believe in an afterlife, although I am bringing a change of underwear.
        Woody Allen

If there is any truth to reincarnation, this must be my first trip through,
'cause I don't recognize anything.
        Hoyt Axton

He hoped and prayed that there wasn't an afterlife. Then he realized there was a contradiction involved here and merely hoped that there wasn't an afterlife.
        Douglas Adams

The last enemy that shall be destroyed is death.
        Bible, 1Corinthians 15:26

We feel and know that we are eternal.
> Baruch de Spinoza

All men think all men mortal but themselves.
> Edward Young

All argument is against it; but all belief is for it.
> Samuel Johnson, on the afterlife

It's all the same to me, I'm already in paradise.
> Moro Dante Spada, a Corsican bandit, upon being condemned to death

The average man, who does not know what to do with his life, wants another one which shall be endless.
> Anatole France

One world at a time.
> Henry David Thoreau, when asked about the hereafter

Age

Age is a high price to pay for maturity.
> Tom Stoppard

What I look forward to is continued immaturity followed by death.
> Dave Barry

Inside every older person is a younger person wondering what the hell happened.
> Cora Harvey Armstrong

Aging seems to be the only available way to live a long life.
> Daniel Francois Esprit Auber

Age is not a particularly interesting subject. Anyone can get old. All you have to do is live long enough.
> Groucho Marx

Old age is not so bad when you consider the alternatives.
> Maurice Chevalier

If you live to be one hundred, you've got it made. Very few people die past that age.
> George Burns

One has only to grow older to become more tolerant. I see no fault that I might not have committed myself.
> Johann Wolfgang von Goethe

A man is not old until regrets take the place of dreams.
John Barrymore

None are so old as those who have outlived enthusiasm.
Henry David Thoreau

The secret to staying young is to live honestly, eat slowly, and lie about your age.
Lucille Ball

How old would you be if you didn't know how old you were?
Leroy (Satchel) Paige

To me, old age is always fifteen years older than I am.
Bernard M. Baruch

I can't see the lines I used to think I could read between.
Brian Eno

The first forty years of life give us the text; the next thirty supply the commentary.
Arthur Schopenhauer

Age imprints more wrinkles in the mind than it does on the face.
Michel de Montaigne

At age 50 everyone has the face he deserves.
George Orwell

The man who views the world at 50 the same as he did at 20 has wasted 30 years of his life.
Muhammad Ali

Age is no mark of merit unless you do something constructive with it.
Irving Berlin

Few people know how to be old.
François duc de la Rochefoucauld

Old age is a shipwreck.
Charles de Gaulle

Old age is no place for sissies.
Bette Davis

Old age comes at a bad time.
Sue Banducci

Growing old is no more than a bad habit which a busy man has no time to form.
André Maurois

We are not limited by our old age; we are liberated by it.
Stu Mittleman

The more sand that has escaped from the hourglass of our life, the clearer we should see through it.
Jean Paul Sartre

Youth is a gift of nature, but age is a work of art.
Garrison Kanin

We grow neither better or worse as we get old, but more like ourselves.
May L. Becker

I'm old enough to be living in the future I was warned about.
Myron Krueger

We don't stop playing because we grow old; we grow old because we stop playing.
George Bernard Shaw

Youth has no age.
Pablo Picasso

We are always the same age inside.
Gertrude Stein

Adults are obsolete children.
Doctor Seuss

Alcohol

An alcoholic is someone you don't like who drinks as much as you do.
Dylan Thomas

You're not drunk if you can lie on the floor without holding on.
Dean Martin

I've never been drunk but often I've been overserved.
George Gobel

I'm not as think as you drunk I am.
Mega Jones

Bacchus hath drowned more men than Neptune.
Dr. Thomas Fuller

It is sweet to drink but bitter to pay for.
 Irish Proverb

Drunkenness is nothing but voluntary madness.
 Seneca

First you take a drink, then the drink takes a drink, then the drink takes you.
 F. Scott Fitzgerald

One martini is all right, two is too many, three is not enough.
 James Thurber

I'm an occasional drinker, the kind of guy who goes out for a beer and wakes up in Singapore with a full beard.
 Raymond Chandler

Even though a number of people have tried, no one has yet found a way to drink for a living.
 Jean Kerr

I only drink to steady my nerves. Sometimes I'm so steady I don't move for months.
 W.C. Fields

Alcohol is the anesthesia by which we endure the operation of life.
 George Bernard Shaw

When you were drunk, the world was still out there, but at least it didn't have you by the throat.
 Charles Bukowski

Drink moderately, for drunkenness neither keeps a secret, nor observes a promise.
 Miguel de Cervantes

There is nothing wrong with sobriety in moderation.
 John Ciardi

It's better to be functionally drunk than dysfunctionally sober.
 Hunter S. Thompson

I drink to make other people more interesting.
 George Jean Nathan

I have to think hard to name an interesting man who does not drink.
 Richard Burton

Beware of the man who does not drink.
 Proverb

I think a man ought to get drunk at least twice a year just on principle so he won't let himself get snotty about it.
>   Raymond Chandler

I feel sorry for people who don't drink. When they wake up in the morning, that's as good as they're going to feel all day.
>   Frank Sinatra

Always remember that I have taken more out of alcohol than alcohol has taken out of me.
>   Winston Churchill

I hate to advocate drugs, alcohol, violence, or insanity to anyone, but they've always worked for me.
>   Hunter S. Thompson

When I read about the evils of drinking, I gave up reading.
>   Henny Youngman

To alcohol! The cause of... and solution to all of life's problems.
>   Homer Simpson

A woman drove me to drink and I didn't even have the decency to thank her.
>   W.C. Fields

It's a wise man who stays home when he's drunk.
>   Euripides

If you name me a street
Then I'll name you a bar
And I'll walk right through Hell
Just to buy you a jar
>   Shane MacGowan

Over the bottle many a friend is found.
>   Yiddish Proverb

A couple of glasses of champagne, and two strangers have a rich and happy past.
>   Leslie Howard, Intermezzo

One reason I don't drink is that I want to know when I'm having a good time.
>   Lady Astor

To stop drinking...study a drunkard while you are sober.
>   Chinese Proverb

Anger

Anger is an energy.
John Lydon, a.k.a. Johnny Rotten

Anger or hate can be a useful motivating force.
Jenny Holzer

The right to swing my fist ends where the other man's nose begins.
Oliver Wendell Holmes

Never fight an inanimate object.
P.J. O'Rourke

Don't ever slam the door; you might want to go back.
Don Herold

Sometimes a scream is better than a thesis.
Ralph Waldo Emerson

Holding on to anger is like grasping a hot coal with the intent of throwing it at someone else; you are the one who gets burned.
Buddha

Anger is as a stone cast into a wasp's nest.
Malabar Proverb

Be angry, and yet do not sin; do not let the sun go down on your anger.
Bible, Ephesians 4:26

Never go to bed angry, stay up and fight.
Phyllis Diller

Don't get mad, get even.
Joseph Patrick Kennedy

Anger is never without a reason, but seldom a good one.
Benjamin Franklin

Anger cannot be dishonest.
George R. Bach

Anger can be an expensive luxury.
Italian Proverb

Anger is a short madness.
Horace

He who angers you conquers you.
Elizabeth Kenny

You can tell the size of a man by the size of the thing that makes him mad.
Adali Stevenson

Many people lose their tempers merely from seeing you keep yours.
Frank Moore Colby

No person is important enough to make me angry.
Carlos Castaneda

Whatever is begun in anger ends in shame.
Benjamin Franklin

A quick temper will make a fool of you soon enough.
Bruce Lee

Anger ends in cruelty.
Indian Proverb

If you are patient in one moment of anger, you will escape a hundred days of sorrow.
Chinese Proverb

Whenever you are angry, be assured that it is not only a present evil,
but that you have increased a habit.
Epictetus

The best cure for anger is delay.
Seneca

Speak when you are angry and you will make the best speech you will ever regret.
Ambrose Bierce

An angry man opens his mouth and shuts his eyes.
Cato

Beware the fury of a patient man.
John Dryden

When angry, count four; when very angry, swear.
Mark Twain

Never forget what a man says to you when he is angry.
Henry Ward Beecher

When anger comes, wisdom goes.
Hindu Proverb

Usually when people are sad, they don't do anything. They just cry over their condition. But when they get angry, they bring about a change.
Malcolm X

Somebody's got to be angry or nothing gets fixed.
Carl Hiaasen

We boil at different degrees.
Ralph Waldo Emerson

Art

Art is not a thing; it is a way.
Elbert G. Hubbard

Art is not a pastime but a priesthood.
Jean Cocteau

Art is Holy Spirit breathing through your soul.
Jack Kerouac

Art attracts us only by what it reveals of our most secret self.
Jean-Luc Godard

Art is not a mirror. Art is a hammer.
Bertolt Brecht

If I could tell you what it meant, there would be no point in dancing it.
Isadora Duncan

The essence of all beautiful art, all great art, is gratitude.
Friedrich Nietzsche

It is only by going too far that you can hope to break the mould and do something new. Art is a question of going too far.
Francis Bacon

Art demands of us that we never stand still.
Ludwig van Beethoven

One always has to spoil a picture a little bit, in order to finish it.
Eugène Delacroix

Art, like morality, consists of drawing the line somewhere.
G.K. Chesterton

Art is the sex of the imagination.
George Jean Nathan

The essence of all art is to have pleasure in giving pleasure
Mikhail Baryshnikov

The first mistake of Art is to assume that it's serious.
Lester Bangs

The goal of life is rapture. Art is the way we experience.
Joseph Campbell

Art is not a handicraft, it is the transmission of feeling the artist has experienced.
Leo Tolstoy

A painting is good not because it looks like something, but because it feels
like something.
Phil Duke

Art is the objectification of feeling.
Suzanne K. Langer

A work of art which did not begin in emotion is not art.
Paul Cézanne

All art is a challenge to despair.
E.C. Bentley

Art is a collaboration between God and the artist, and the less the artist does
the better.
André Gide

The true work of art is but a shadow of the divine perfection.
Michelangelo

Art is too superior to life to be satisfied with copying it.
Marcel Proust

The difference between Art and Life is that Art is more bearable.
Charles Bukowski

Life beats down and crushes the soul and art reminds you that you have one.
Stella Adler

Art is the stored honey of the human soul, gathered on wings of misery
and travail.
Theodore Dreiser

Art washes away from the soul the dust of everyday life.
Pablo Picasso

Art teaches nothing, except the significance of life.
Henry Miller

The object of art is to give life a shape.
Jean Anouilh

Art is the affirmation of life.
Alfred Stieglitz

Art is uncompromising, and life is full of compromises.
Gunther Grass

Art should never try to be popular. The public should try to make itself artistic.
Oscar Wilde

The only way art lives is through the experience of the observer. The reality of art begins in the eyes of the beholder, through imagination, invention, and confrontation.
Keith Haring

I am for an art that is political-erotic-mystical, that does something else than sit on its ass in a museum.
Claes Oldenburg

True art is selfish and perverse – it will not submit to the mold of flattery.
Ludwig van Beethoven

Art is meant to disturb, science reassures.
Georges Braque

I've suffered for my art. Now it's your turn.
Marshall Crenshaw

Creativity is allowing yourself to make mistakes. Art is knowing which ones to keep.
Scott Adams

Perfection is achieved, not when there is nothing more to add, but when there is nothing left to take away.
Antoine de Saint-Exupéry

I choose a block of marble and chop off whatever I don't need.
Auguste Rodin, when asked how he made his remarkable statues

In art economy is always beauty.
Henry James

Art is the science of beauty.
James McNeill Whistler

Art is the only way to run away without leaving home.
Twyla Tharp

Art enables us to find ourselves and lose ourselves at the same time.
Thomas Merton

Art flourishes where there is a sense of adventure.
Alfred North Whitehead

Every great work of art has two faces, one toward its own time and one toward the future, toward eternity.
Daniel Barenboim

Art is the signature of civilizations.
Beverly Sills

Art is a form of catharsis.
Dorothy Parker

Art is either plagiarism or revolution.
Paul Gauguin

Good artists copy; great artists steal.
Pablo Picasso

Love art. Of all lies, it is the least untrue.
Gustave Flaubert

Art is anything you can get away with.
Marshall McLuhan

What is art but a way of seeing?
Thomas Berger

The artist's vocation is to send light into the human heart.
Robert Schumann

Where the spirit does not work with the hand, there is no art.
Leonardo da Vinci

The arts are not a luxury. They're how we know we're not alone.
W.O. Mitchell

Artists

A plausible mission of artists is to make people appreciate being alive at least a little bit.
>Kurt Vonnegut

The defining function of the artist is to cherish consciousness.
>Max Eastman

An intellectual is a man who says a simple thing in a difficult way, an artist is a man who says a difficult thing in a simple way.
>Charles Bukowski

The position of the artist is humble. He is essentially a channel.
>Piet Mondrian

The artist is not there to be at one with the world, he is there to transform it.
>Anaïs Nin

The artist is a dreamer consenting to dream of the actual world.
>George Santayana

An artist is not paid for his labor but for his vision.
>James McNeill Whistler

If you don't have the nerve to be a homosexual and you really want to upset your parents, the least you can do is go into the arts.
>Kurt Vonnegut

The artist can within limits make what he likes of his life. It is only the artist, and maybe the criminal, who can make his own.
>W. Somerset Maugham

An artist is a person who has invented an artist.
>Harold Rosenberg

An artist is the one who kids himself most gracefully.
>Don Van Vliet, a.k.a. Captain Beefheart

It is so much worse to be a mediocre artist than to be a mediocre post office clerk.
>Rudolf Bing

The artist finds a greater pleasure in painting than in having completed the picture.
>Seneca

A creative artist works on his composition because he was not satisfied with his previous one.
>Dmitri Shostakovich

An artist never really finishes his work; he merely abandons it.
> Paul Valéry

In the cycle of a great civilization, the artist begins as priest, and ends as a clown or buffoon.
> Malcolm Muggeridge

The first prerogative of an artist in any medium is to make a fool of himself.
> Pauline Kael

The artist produces for the liberation of his soul. It is his nature to create as it is the nature of water to run downhill.
> W. Somerset Maugham

I passionately hate the idea of being with it, I think an artist has always to be out of step with his time.
> Orson Welles

No artist is ahead of his time. He is his time. It is just that others are behind the time.
> Martha Graham

An artist must know how to convince others of the truth of his lies.
> Pablo Picasso

Never trust the artist. Trust the tale.
> D.H. Lawrence

It is very good advice to believe only what an artist does, rather than what he says about his work.
> David Hockney

Every child is an artist. The problem is how to remain an artist once he grows up.
> Pablo Picasso

The progress of an artist is a continual self-sacrifice, a continual extinction of personality.
> T.S. Eliot

To be an artist means never to avert one's eyes.
> Akiro Kurosawa

I always suspect an artist who is successful before he is dead.
> John Murray Gibbon

The job of the artist is always to deepen the mystery.
> Francis Bacon

Attitude

The greatest discovery of my generation is that a human being can alter his life by altering his attitude.
> William James

Could we change our attitude, we should not only see life differently, but life itself would come to be different.
> Katherine Mansfield

I don't think of all the misery, but of all the beauty that remains.
> Anne Frank

Attitudes are more important than facts.
> Norman Vincent Peale

Do not take life seriously. You will never get out of it alive.
> Elbert G. Hubbard

The reason angels can fly is that they take themselves so lightly.
> G.K. Chesterton

There is no sadder sight than a young pessimist.
> Mark Twain

Most human beings have an almost infinite capacity for taking things for granted.
> Aldous Huxley

Nothing can stop the man with the right mental attitude from achieving his goal; nothing on earth can help the man with the wrong mental attitude.
> Thomas Jefferson

The only disability in life is a bad attitude.
> Scott Hamilton

Dare to be naïve.
> R. Buckminster Fuller

I have a simple philosophy. Fill what's empty. Empty what's full. Scratch where it itches.
> Alice Roosevelt Longworth

There is less to this than meets the eye.
> Tallulah Bankhead

Stagger onward rejoicing.
> W.H. Auden

Of course I'm an optimist. What's the point of being anything else?
　　Winston Churchill

Be curious always! For knowledge will not acquire you; you must acquire it.
　　Sudie Back

Never lose a holy curiosity.
　　Albert Einstein

The cure for boredom is curiosity. There is no cure for curiosity.
　　Dorothy Parker

I am never bored anywhere: being bored is an insult to oneself.
　　Jules Renard

Nothing is interesting if you're not interested.
　　Helen MacInness

A positive attitude may not solve all your problems, but it will annoy enough people
to make it worth the effort.
　　Herm Albright

I like a man who grins when he fights.
　　Winston Churchill

To the man who only has a hammer, everything he encounters begins to look
like a nail.
　　Abraham H. Maslow

Think you can or think you can't, either way you will be right.
　　Henry Ford

Act as if what you do makes a difference. It does.
　　William James

We either make ourselves miserable, or we make ourselves strong. The amount
of work is the same.
　　Carlos Castaneda

Expect nothing; be prepared for anything.
　　Samurai Saying

The last of the human freedoms is to choose one's attitudes.
　　Victor Frankl

Never let yesterday use up too much of today.
　　Will Rogers

Some people walk in the rain, others just get wet.
Roger Miller

No life is so hard that you can't make it easier by the way you take it.
Ellen Glasgow

Awareness

You can observe a lot by just watching.
Yogi Berra

Perception is attention.
Novalis

There is no such thing as talent, only awareness.
Chogyam Trungpa

Life is in session. Are you present?
B. Copeland

Presence is more than just being there.
Malcolm Forbes

Do not look back in anger, or forward in fear, but around in awareness.
James Thurber

In the name of God, stop a moment, cease your work, look around you.
Leo Tolstoy

The aim of life is to live, and to live means to be aware, joyously, drunkenly,
serenely, divinely aware.
Henry Miller

The ultimate value of life depends upon awareness, and the power of contemplation
rather than upon mere survival.
Aristotle

If the doors of perception were cleansed, every thing would appear to man
as it is, infinite.
William Blake

To the dull mind all of nature is leaden. To the illumined mind the whole world
burns and sparkles with light.
Ralph Waldo Emerson

Our awareness is all that is alive and maybe sacred in any of us. Everything else about us is dead machinery.
>Kurt Vonnegut

The present contains all that there is. It is holy ground.
>Alfred North Whitehead

Be here now.
>Baba Ram Dass

The living moment is everything.
>D.H. Lawrence

Right now a moment of time is passing by! We must become that moment.
>Paul Cézanne

Compared to what we ought to be, we are half awake.
>William James

Only that day dawns to which we are awake.
>Henry David Thoreau

If I were to begin life again, I should want it as it was. I would only open my eyes a little more.
>Jules Renard

Beginnings and Endings

The world is round and the place which may seem like the end may also be only the beginning.
>Ivy Baker

With the possible exception of the equator, everything begins somewhere.
>Peter Fleming

He who begins many things finishes but few.
>Italian Proverb

The great majority of men are bundles of beginnings.
>Ralph Waldo Emerson

There will come a time when you believe everything is finished. That will be the beginning.
>Louis L'Amour

When the way comes to an end, then change. Having changed, you pass through.
    I Ching

Better is the end of a thing than the beginning thereof.
    Bible, Ecclesiastes 7:8

All's well that ends well.
    William Shakespeare

In the beginning you must subject yourself to the influence of nature. You must be able to walk firmly on the ground before you start walking on a tightrope.
    Henri Matisse

In soloing, as in other activities, it is far easier to start something that it is to finish it.
    Amelia Earhart

Begin at the beginning and go on till you come to the end; then stop.
    Lewis Carroll

Whenever a thing is done for the first time, it releases a little demon.
    Dave Sim

A good beginning makes a good end.
    English Proverb

In my beginning is my end.
    T.S. Eliot

Every step is an end, and every step is a fresh beginning.
    Johann Wolfgang von Goethe

The beginnings and the endings of all human undertakings are untidy.
    John Galsworthy

A story should have a beginning, a middle, and an end... but not necessarily in that order.
    Jean-Luc Godard

Whatever you can do or dream you can, begin it. Boldness has genius, power and magic in it.
    Johann Wolfgang von Goethe

All glory comes from daring to begin.
    Eugene F. Ware

Things are always at their best in the beginning.
    Blaise Pascal

We shall never cease from exploration, And the end of all our exploring will be to arrive where we started, And know the place for the first time.
> T.S. Eliot

The truth is that the beginning of anything and its end are alike touching.
> Yoshida Kenkō

Well begun is half done.
> Aristotle

Every beginning is a consequence – every beginning ends something.
> Paul Valéry

Every exit is an entry somewhere else.
> Tom Stoppard

Chance

There is a meaning in each play of chance.
> Sri Aurobindo

Chance, to be precise, is a leap, provides a leap out of reach of one's own grasp of oneself.
> John Cage

Chance favors only those who court her.
> Charles Nicolle

We are ruled by chance but never have enough patience to accept its despotism.
> Edward Dahlberg

Chance is a word void of sense; nothing can exist without a cause.
> Voltaire

No victor believes in chance.
> Friedrich Nietzsche

I figure you have the same chance of winning the lottery whether you play or not.
> Fran Lebowitz

In the shaping of a life, chance and the ability to respond to chance are everything.
> Eric Hoffer

Chance makes a football of man's life.
> Seneca

Chance does nothing that has not been prepared beforehand.
    Alexis de Tocqueville

Did you ever observe to whom the accidents happen? Chance favors only the prepared mind.
    Louis Pasteur

Chance fights ever on the side of the prudent.
    Euripides

One chance is all you need.
    Jesse Owens

A wise man turns chance into good fortune.
    Dr. Thomas Fuller

Chance is always powerful. Let your hook be always cast; in the pool where you least expect it, there will be a fish.
    Ovid

Chance is perhaps the pseudonym of God when he does not wish to sign his work.
    Anatole France

Change

Life goes into new forms.
    Neal Cassady

There is nothing permanent except change.
    Heraclitus

It takes a deep commitment to change and an even deeper commitment to grow.
    Ralph Ellison

It is not the strongest of the species that survive, nor the most intelligent, but the one most responsive to change.
    Charles Darwin

Only in growth, reform, and change, paradoxically enough, is true security to be found.
    Anne Morrow Lindbergh

To change your life: start immediately; do it flamboyantly; no exceptions.
    William James

Never doubt that a small group of thoughtful, committed citizens can change the world; indeed, it's the only thing that ever has.
>   Margaret Mead

I wanted to change the world. But I have found that the only thing one can be sure of changing is oneself.
>   Aldous Huxley

Consider how hard it is to change yourself and you'll understand what little chance you have in trying to change others.
>   Jacob M. Braude

Those who cannot change their minds cannot change anything.
>   George Bernard Shaw

If you want to make enemies, try to change something.
>   Woodrow Wilson

Change and growth take place when a person has risked himself and dares to become involved with experimenting with his own life.
>   Herbert Otto

All change is not growth; all movement is not forward.
>   Ellen Glasgow

I can be changed by what happens to me. I refuse to be reduced by it.
>   Maya Angelou

You have to endure what you can't change.
>   Marie de France

Only I can change my life. No one can do it for me.
>   Carol Burnett

We must become the change we want to see.
>   Mahatma Gandhi

Change your thoughts and you change your world.
>   Norman Vincent Peale

The people who are crazy enough to think they can change the world, are the ones who do.
>   Think Different, Apple 1997 television commercial

Not everything that is faced can be changed. But nothing can be changed until it is faced.
>   James Baldwin

When you blame others, you give up your power to change.
Dr. Robert Anthony

To mutate faster.
Igor Stravinsky, when asked why he moved to New York City at age 69

Change is not merely necessary to life, it is life.
Alvin Toffler

They always say time changes things, but you actually have to change them yourself.
Andy Warhol

There is nothing constant in the universe. All ebb and flow, and every shape that's born, bears in its womb the seeds of change.
Ovid

A wave of your hand can change the universe.
Tali Nadav

Everything flows and nothing stays.
Heraclitus

When the way comes to an end, then change. Having changed, you pass through.
I Ching

When one door is closed many more are opened.
Bob Marley

To improve is to change; to be perfect is to change often.
Winston Churchill

The thing about change is that it's not permanent.
Tracy Clavin

Things do not change; we change.
Henry David Thoreau

People change and forget to tell each other.
Lillian Hellman

The universe is change; our life is what our thoughts make it.
Marcus Aurelius

We must always change, renew, rejuvenate ourselves; otherwise we harden.
Johann Wolfgang von Goethe

Without change, something sleeps inside us, and seldom awakens. The sleeper must awaken.
> Frank Herbert

When you're through changing, you're through.
> Bruce Barton

If you don't like what you're doing, you can always pick up your needle and move to another groove.
> Timothy Leary

The only consistent people are the dead.
> Aldous Huxley

Only the wisest and the stupidest of men never change.
> Confucius

You could not step twice into the same rivers; for other waters are ever flowing on to you.
> Heraclitus

Character

Character is destiny.
> Heraclitus

Character is simply habit long continued.
> Plutarch

Character may be manifested in the great moments, but it is made in the small ones.
> Phillips Brooks

People pay for what they do, and still more, for what they have allowed themselves to become. And they pay for it simply: by the lives they lead.
> James Baldwin

If a man has no enemies, he has no character.
> Frank Sinatra

When the character of a man is not clear to you, look at his friends.
> Haitian Proverb

Character is a diamond that scratches every other stone.
> Cyrus A. Bartol

Talent develops in tranquility, character in the full current of human life.
Johann Wolfgang von Goethe

People grow through experience if they meet life honestly and courageously. This is how character is built.
Eleanor Roosevelt

Character cannot be developed in ease and quiet. Only through experience of trial and suffering can the soul be strengthened, vision cleared, ambition inspired, and success achieved.
Helen Keller

A man of character finds a special attractiveness in difficulty, since it is only by coming to grips with difficulty that he can realize his potentialities.
Charles De Gaulle

People seem not to see that their opinion of the world is also a confession of character.
Ralph Waldo Emerson

The real character of a man is found out by his amusements.
Sir Joshua Reynolds

Nothing shows a man's character more than what he laughs at.
Johann Wolfgang von Goethe

Few women and fewer men have enough character to be idle.
E.V. Lucas

Every man has three characters – that which he exhibits, that which he has, and that which he thinks he has.
Alphonse Karr

Many a man's reputation would not know his character if they met on the street.
Elbert G. Hubbard

Character is like a tree and reputation like its shadow. The shadow is what we think of it; the tree is the real thing.
Abraham Lincoln

The cobra will bite you whether you call it cobra or Mr. Cobra.
Indian Proverb

To live outside the law a man must be honest.
Bob Dylan

The childhood shows the man, as morning shows the day.
John Milton

The measure of a man's real character is what he would do if he knew he would never be found out.
> Thomas Babington Macaulay

Character is doing what's right when nobody's looking.
> J.C. Watts

Happiness is not the end of life; character is.
> Henry Ward Beecher

Be more concerned with your character than with your reputation. Your character is what you really are while your reputation is merely what others think you are.
> Dale Carnegie

No change of circumstances can repair a defect of character.
> Ralph Waldo Emerson

A man's character is his guardian divinity.
> Heraclitus

No man can climb out beyond the limitations of his own character.
> John Morley

Ability may get you to the top, but it takes character to keep you there.
> John R. Wooden

It takes more strength of character to withstand good fortune than bad.
> François duc de la Rochefoucauld

Character is much easier kept than recovered.
> Thomas Paine

Character begins to form at the first pinch of anxiety about ourselves.
> Yevgeny Yevtushenko

Development of character consists solely in moving toward self-sufficiency.
> Quentin Crisp

Obedience.
> Henrich Böll, when asked what he viewed as the basic flaw of the German character

I am a deeply superficial person.
> Andy Warhol

Those are my principles. If you don't like them I have others.
> Groucho Marx

Comedy and Humor

Comedy is tragedy plus time.
    Carol Burnett

All tragedies are finished by a death. All comedies are ended by a marriage.
    Lord Byron

When a thing is funny, search it carefully for a hidden truth.
    George Bernard Shaw

The best thing about humor is that it shows people that they're not alone.
    Sid Caesar

Laughter is the closest distance between two people.
    Victor Borge

Laughter is the language of the soul.
    Pablo Neruda

Laughter is carbonated holiness.
    Anne Lamott

The gods, too, are fond of a joke.
    Aristotle

Time spent laughing is time spent with the gods.
    Japanese Proverb

Jesters do often prove prophets.
    William Shakespeare

Humor is an affirmation of dignity, a declaration of man's superiority to all that befalls him.
    Roman Gary

If I had no sense of humor, I would long ago have committed suicide.
    Mahatma Gandhi

Total absence of humor renders life impossible.
    Colette

If you lose the power to laugh, you lose the power to think.
    Clarence Darrow

Analyzing humor is like dissecting a frog: Nobody really enjoys it and the frog generally dies as a result.
    E.B. White

Everything is funny, as long as it's happening to somebody else.
  Will Rogers

Laugh at yourself first, before anyone else can.
  Elsa Maxwell

Anyone without a sense of humor is at the mercy of everyone else.
  William Rose Wallace

Humor distorts nothing, and only false gods are laughed off their earthly pedestals.
  Agnes Repplier

When you can laugh at yourself, there is enlightenment.
  Shunryu Suzuki Roshi

He deserves Paradise who makes his companions laugh.
  The Koran

Comedy is an escape, not from the truth but from despair; a narrow escape into faith.
  Christopher Fry

Humor is a prelude to faith and laughter is the beginning of prayer.
  Reinhold Niebuhr

Nobody ever died of laughter.
  Max Beerbohm

Dying is easy. Comedy is difficult.
  Edmund Kean

A man's got to take a lot of punishment to write a really funny book.
  Ernest Hemingway

Humor is by far the most significant activity of the human brain.
  Edward de Bono

The world is a comedy to those who think, a tragedy to those who feel.
  Horace Walpole

Humor is mankind's greatest blessing.
  Mark Twain

Always laugh when you can. It is cheap medicine.
  Lord Byron

The most wasted day of all is that in which we have not laughed.
  Sébastien Chamfort

The test of a real comedian is whether you laugh at him before he opens his mouth.
George Jean Nathan

There's a hell of a distance between wisecracking and wit. Wit has truth in it; wisecracking is simply calisthenics with words.
Dorothy Parker

Levity is the soul of wit.
Carlton

Wit is educated insolence.
Aristotle

You can pretend to be serious; you can't pretend to be witty.
Sacha Guitry

The only honest art form is laughter, comedy. You can't fake it.
Lenny Bruce

There is only one step from the sublime to the ridiculous.
Napoleon Bonaparte

Tell me what you're laughing at and I shall tell you who you are.
Johann Wolfgang von Goethe

Among those whom I like or admire, I can find no common denominator, but among those whom I love, I can: all of them make me laugh.
W.H. Auden

A joke is a very serious thing.
Winston Churchill

Comedy is simply a funny way of being serious.
Peter Ustinov

There are things that are so serious that you can only joke about them.
Werner Heisenberg

A sense of humor is just common sense dancing.
Clive James

When I am very sad I make a comedy, and when I am very happy, I make a serious drama.
Billy Wilder

All my humor is based upon destruction and despair.
Lenny Bruce

Humor is just another defense against the universe.
  Mel Brooks

The kind of humor I like is the thing that makes me laugh for five seconds and think for ten minutes.
  William Davis

There's so much comedy on television. Does that cause comedy in the streets?
  Dick Cavett

Our comedies are not to be laughed at.
  Samuel Goldwyn, on his MGM productions

The human race has one really effective weapon, and that is laughter.
  Mark Twain

In the end, everything is a gag.
  Charlie Chaplin

Communication

Human speech is like a cracked kettle on which we tap crude rhythms for bears to dance to, while we long to make music that will melt the stars.
  Gustave Flaubert

Good communication is as stimulating as black coffee and just as hard to sleep after.
  Anne Morrow Lindbergh

The most important thing in communication is to hear what isn't being said.
  Peter F. Drucker

I like to listen. I have learned a great deal from listening carefully. Most people never listen.
  Ernest Hemingway

No one really listens to anyone else, and if you try it for a while you will see why.
  Mignon McLaughlin

Sixty percent of human communication is miscommunication.
  De Rerum Comoedia

Be obscure clearly.
  E.B. White

Every improvement in communication makes the bore more terrible.
  Frank Moore Colby

The best way to become boring is to say everything.
Voltaire

To think justly, we must understand what others mean: to know the value of our thoughts, we must try their effect on other minds.
William Hazlitt

Most conversations are simply monologues delivered in the presence of witnesses.
Margaret Millar

Two monologues do not make a dialogue.
Jeff Daly

It was impossible to get a conversation going, everybody was talking too much.
Yogi Berra

There is nothing so annoying as to have two people go right on talking when you're interrupting.
Mark Twain

To express the most difficult matters clearly and intelligently is to strike coins out of pure gold.
Emanuel Geibel

Communication is most complete when it proceeds from the smallest number of words, and indeed of syllables.
Jacques Barzun

Too much agreement kills a chat.
Eldridge Cleaver

One way to prevent conversation from being boring is to say the wrong thing.
Frank Sheed

When you talk, you repeat what you already know; when you listen, you often learn something.
Jared Sparks

No one would talk much in society if they knew how often they misunderstood others.
Johann Wolfgang von Goethe

Everything that needs to be said has already been said. But since no one was listening, everything must be said again.
André Gide

The greatest problem of communication is the illusion that it has been accomplished.
George Bernard Shaw

Compassion

Love and compassion are necessities, not luxuries. Without them, humanity cannot survive.
>> Tenzin Gyatso, 14th Dalai Lama

If your compassion does not include yourself, it is incomplete.
>> Jack Kornfield

The depth of your compassion lies in your ability to forgive yourself.
>> Mark Graham

To develop understanding, you have to practice looking at all living things with the eyes of compassion.
>> Thich Nhat Hanh

Compassion is the keen awareness of the interdependence of all things.
>> Thomas Merton

Until he extends his circle of compassion to all living things, man will not himself find peace.
>> Albert Schweitzer

It is much easier to show compassion to animals. They are never wicked.
>> Haile Selassie

Compassion is daring to acknowledge our own destiny so that we might move forward together.
>> Henri Nouwen

To grow old is to pass from passion to compassion.
>> Albert Camus

Compassion is the basis of morality.
>> Arthur Schopenhauer

I feel the capacity to care is the thing which gives life its deepest significance.
>> Pablo Casals

Fill your mind with compassion.
>> Buddha

He who feels no compassion will become insane.
>> Hasidic Saying

Man may dismiss compassion from his heart, but God never will.
>> William Cowper

Compassion is the only one of the human emotions the Lord permitted Himself and it has carried the divine flavor ever since.
Dagobert Runes

The dew of compassion is a tear.
Lord Byron

Make no judgements where you have no compassion.
Anne McCaffrey

The value of compassion cannot be over-emphasized. Anyone can criticize. It takes a true believer to be compassionate.
Arthur H. Stainback

If you want others to be happy, practice compassion. If you want to be happy, practice compassion.
Tenzin Gyatso, 14th Dalai Lama

Compassion is the antitoxin of the soul: where there is compassion even the most poisonous impulses remain relatively harmless.
Eric Hoffer

Conduct

First of all, do no harm.
Latin Proverb

A man should not strive to eliminate his complexes, but to live in accord with them; they are legitimately what directs his conduct in the world.
Sigmund Freud

A man's behavior is the index of the man, and his discourse is the index of his understanding.
Ali Ibn-Abi-Talib

I believe I have found the link between animals and civilized man. It is us.
Konrad Lorenz

He who makes a beast of himself gets rid of the pain of being a man.
Samuel Johnson

That ain't tactics, baby. That's just the beast in me.
Elvis Presley, Jailhouse Rock

If not for the beast within us we would be castrated angels.
Hermann Hesse

36

A man does not have to be an angel in order to be saint.
    Albert Schweitzer

I don't say we all ought to misbehave, but we ought to look as if we could.
    Orson Welles

Give me continence and chastity, but not yet.
    Saint Augustine

What demon possessed me that I behaved so well.
    Henry David Thoreau

Rudeness is a weak person's attempt at strength.
    J. Matthew Casey

Never offend people with style when you can offend them with substance.
    Sam Brown

The true measure of a man is how he treats someone who can do him absolutely no good.
    Samuel Johnson

Manners are just a formal expression of how you treat people.
    Molly Ivins

Manners maketh man.
    William of Wykeham

Politeness is just a matter of phrasing.
    L.J. Stafford

Politeness has won more victories than logic ever has.
    Josh Billings

My problem lies in reconciling my gross habits with my net income.
    Errol Flynn

My moral standing is lying down.
    Trent Reznor

Conduct is three-fourths of our life and its largest concern.
    Matthew Arnold

In great matters, men behave as they are expected to; in little ones, as they would naturally.
    Sébastien Chamfort

The conduct of our lives is the true mirror of our doctrine.
Michel de Montaigne

The trouble with being punctual is that nobody's there to appreciate it.
Franklin P. Jones

Fine conduct is always spontaneous.
Seneca

Great minds discuss ideas; average minds discuss events; small minds discuss people.
Eleanor Roosevelt

If you haven't got anything nice to say about anybody, come sit next to me.
Alice Roosevelt Longworth

Don't talk about yourself; it will be done when you leave.
Wilson Mizner

It isn't what they say about you, it's what they whisper.
Errol Flynn

Never say anything on the phone that you wouldn't want your mother to hear at your trial.
Sydney Biddle Barrows

As I grow older, I pay less attention to what men say. I just watch what they do.
Andrew Carnegie

Example is not the main thing in influencing others. It is the only thing.
Albert Schweitzer

Nothing is true, everything is permitted.
Hassan I Sabbah, assassin

Conformity

If they give you ruled paper, write the other way.
Juan Ramón Jiménez

Hell, there are no rules here – we're trying to accomplish something.
Thomas Edison

You are remembered for the rules you break.
Douglas MacArthur

There are some things one can only achieve by a deliberate leap in the opposite direction.
> Franz Kafka

It is opposition that makes us productive.
> Johann Wolfgang von Goethe

We forfeit three quarters of our lives to be like other people.
> Arthur Shopenhauer

Always be a first rate version of your self instead of a second rate version of someone else.
> Judy Garland

We are discreet sheep; we wait to see how the drove is going, and then go with the drove.
> Mark Twain

The dissenter is every human being at those moments of his life when he resigns momentarily from the herd and thinks for himself.
> Archibald MacLeish

Conformity is the ape of harmony.
> Ralph Waldo Emerson

Abnormal, adj. Not conforming to standard. In matters of thought and conduct, to be independent is to be abnormal, to be abnormal is to be detested.
> Ambrose Bierce, The Devil's Dictionary

Men are created different; they lose their social freedom and their individual autonomy in seeking to become like each other.
> David Riesman

Don't say yes until I finish talking.
> Darryl F. Zanuck

I resign. I wouldn't want to belong to any club that would have me as a member.
> Groucho Marx

Gentlemen, include me out.
> Samuel Goldwyn

We are half ruined by conformity, but we should be wholly ruined without it.
> Charles Dudley Warner

How glorious it is, and also how painful, to be an exception.
> Alfred de Musset

Do not follow where the path may lead. Go, instead, where there is no path and leave a trail.
Ralph Waldo Emerson

Conformity is the jailer of freedom and the enemy of growth.
John F. Kennedy

That which has always been accepted by everyone, everywhere, is almost certain to be false.
Paul Valéry

The conventional view serves to protect us from the painful job of thinking.
John Kenneth Galbraith

If everybody is thinking alike, then somebody isn't thinking.
George S. Patton

It is not worth an intelligent man's time to be in the majority. By definition, there are already enough people to do that.
G.H. Hardy

Whenever you find yourself on the side of the majority, it is time to pause and reflect.
Mark Twain

Whenever people agree with me I always feel I must be wrong.
Oscar Wilde

A man must consider what a rich realm he abdicates when he becomes a conformist.
Ralph Waldo Emerson

Everything I did in my life that was worthwhile, I caught hell for.
Earl Warren

The nail that sticks up will be hammered down.
Japanese Proverb

Anybody who is any good is different from anybody else.
Felix Frankfurter

Do not fear to be eccentric in opinion, for every opinion now accepted was once eccentric.
Bertrand Russell

Though all men be made of one metal, yet they be not cast all in one mold.
John Lyly

Whoso would be a man must be a nonconformist.
Ralph Waldo Emerson

Why is it that all non-conformists look the same?
Billy Corgan

Men are born equal but they are also born different.
Erich Fromm

The surest way to corrupt a youth is to instruct him to hold in higher esteem those who think alike than those who think differently.
Friedrich Nietzsche

Just think of the tragedy of teaching children not to doubt.
Clarence Darrow

If fifty million people say a foolish thing, it is still a foolish thing.
Anatole France

I don't necessarily agree with everything I say.
Marshall McLuhan

The strongest man in the world is he who stands alone.
Henrik Ibsen

It is better to fail in originality than to succeed in imitation.
Herman Melville

I don't know the key to success, but the key to failure is trying to please everybody.
Bill Cosby

Control

If everything seems under control, you're just not going fast enough.
Mario Andretti

Never let the other fellow set the agenda.
James Baker

If you don't control your mind, someone else will.
John Allston

The only thing worse than a man you can't control, is a man you can.
Margo Kaufman

The bird of paradise alights only on the hand that does not grasp.
John Berry

Once the toothpaste is out of the tube, it is awfully hard to get it back in.
H.R. Halderman

No man is fit to command another that cannot command himself.
William Penn

Nothing gives a person so much advantage over another as to remain always cool and unruffled under all circumstances.
Thomas Jefferson

You cannot always control what goes on outside. But you can always control what goes on inside.
Wayne Dyer

The one thing over which you have absolute control is your own thoughts. It is this that puts you in a position to control your own destiny.
Paul G. Thomas

Of all men's miseries the bitterest is this: to know so much and to have control over nothing.
Herodotus

How can anyone govern a nation that has 246 different kinds of cheese?
Charles De Gaulle

I claim not to have controlled events, but confess plainly that events have controlled me.
Abraham Lincoln

When I grip the wheel too tight, I find I lose control.
Steve Rapson

Courage

With courage you will dare to take risks, have the strength to be compassionate and the wisdom to be humble. Courage is the foundation of integrity.
Keshavan Nair

Life shrinks or expands in proportion to ones' courage.
Anaïs Nin

If you are lucky enough to find a way of life you love, you have to find the courage to live it.
>	John Irving

Everyone has a talent. What is rare is the courage to follow the talent to the dark place where it leads.
>	Erica Jong

Courage doesn't know what's around the corner, but goes around it anyway.
>	Mignon McLaughlin

Courage is like love; it must have hope to nourish it.
>	Napoleon Bonaparte

The greatest test of courage on the earth is to bear defeat without losing heart.
>	Robert G. Ingersoll

Courage is getting away from death by continually coming within an inch of it.
>	G.K. Chesterton

Have the courage to live. Anyone can die.
>	Robert Cody

Cowards die many times; a brave man dies but once.
>	William Shakespeare

Sometimes even to live is an act of courage.
>	Seneca

Real courage is when you know you're licked before you begin, but you begin anyway and see it through no matter what.
>	Harper Lee

One man with courage makes a majority.
>	Andrew Jackson

Courage is what it takes to stand up and speak; courage is also what it takes to sit down and listen.
>	Winston Churchill

Courage is like a muscle. We strengthen it with use.
>	Ruth Gordon

Until the day of his death, no man can be sure if his courage.
>	Jean Anouilh

No one can answer for his courage when he has never been in danger.
>	François duc de la Rochefoucauld

Keep your fears to yourself, but share your courage with others.
Robert Louis Stevenson

I never thought much of the courage of a lion tamer. Inside the cage he is at least safe from people.
George Bernard Shaw

It is easy to be brave from a safe distance.
Aesop

Courage is the first of human qualities because it is the quality which guarantees all others.
Winston Churchill

Without courage you cannot practice any of the other virtues.
Maya Angelou

Courage is not simply one of the virtues, but the form of every virtue at the testing point.
C.S. Lewis

He who loses wealth loses much; he who loses a friend loses more; but he that loses his courage loses all.
Miguel de Cervantes

Courage is resistance to fear, mastery of fear – not absence of fear.
Mark Twain

Courage is not the absence of fear, but rather the judgment that something else is more important than fear.
Ambrose Redmoon

Courage is doing what you're afraid of. There can be no courage unless you're scared.
Eddie Rickenbacker

Courage is being scared to death but saddling up anyway.
John Wayne

Courage is fear that has said its prayers.
Dorothy Bernard

Courage is a kind of salvation.
Plato

Courage is grace under pressure.
Ernest Hemingway

Courage is the price that life exacts for granting peace.
Amelia Earhart

The paradox of courage is that a man must be a little careless of his life even in order to keep it.
G.K. Chesterton

People with courage and character always seem sinister to the rest.
Hermann Hesse

It is curious that physical courage should be so common in the world, and moral courage so rare.
Mark Twain

The only courage that matters is the kind that gets you from one moment to the next.
Mignon McLaughlin

Creativity

You are lost the instant you know what the result will be.
Juan Gris

Creativity is the power to connect the seemingly unconnected.
William Plomer

To think creatively, we must be able to look afresh at what we normally take for granted.
George Kneller

Creativity can solve almost any problem. The creative act, the defeat of habit by originality, overcomes everything.
George Lois

The creative person is more primitive and more cultivated, more destructive, a lot madder and a lot saner, than the average person.
Frank Barron

Creative minds have always been known to survive any kind of bad training.
Anna Freud

The more you reason the less you create.
Raymond Chandler

A hunch is creativity trying to tell you something.
Frank Capra

I invent nothing; I rediscover.
   Auguste Rodin

Creative thought must always contain a random component.
   Gregory Bateson

If it's offbeat or surprising, it's probably useful.
   Wendell Castle

Mistakes are the portals of discovery.
   James Joyce

The first rule of intelligent tinkering is to save all the pieces.
   Aldo Leopald

Men are like trees: each one must put forth the leaf that is created in him.
   Henry Ward Beecher

Every production must resemble its author.
   Miguel de Cervantes

Our inventions mirror our secret wishes.
   Lawrence Durrell

Think before you speak is criticism's motto; speak before you think creation's.
   E.M. Forster

Man unites himself with the world in the process of creation.
   Erich Fromm

A creator needs only one enthusiast to justify him.
   Man Ray

Creativity – It's like driving a car at night. You never see further than your headlights, but you can make the whole trip that way.
   E.L. Doctorow

All men are creative but few are artists.
   Paul Goodman

He who does not know how to create should not know.
   Antonio Porchia

Confidence in nonsense is a requirement for the creative process.
   Unknown

The chief enemy of creativity is good taste.
   Pablo Picasso

The spirit of creation is simply the spirit of contradiction.
Jean Cocteau

The secret to creativity is knowing how to hide your sources.
Albert Einstein

Nothing encourages creativity like the chance to fall flat on one's face.
James D. Finley

You can't wait for inspiration. You have to go after it with a club.
Jack London

Death and Dying

I'm not afraid to die, I just don't want to be there when it happens.
Woody Allen

Always go to other peoples' funerals, otherwise they won't go to yours.
Yogi Berra

The reports of my death have been greatly exaggerated.
Mark Twain

The last enemy that shall be destroyed is death.
Bible, 1 Corinthians 15:26

While I thought that I was learning how to live, I have been learning how to die.
Leonardo da Vinci

To die is landing on some distant shore.
John Dryden

Today is a good day to die.
Sitting Bull

Seeing death as the end of life is like seeing the horizon as the end of the ocean.
David Searls

Death is not extinguishing the light; it is putting out the lamp because the dawn has come.
Rabindranath Tagore

There is no death by natural causes.
Norman O. Brown

Death, the one appointment we all must keep, and for which no time is set.
    Charlie Chan

Death does not sound a trumpet.
    Congolese Proverb

Do not seek death. Death will find you.
    Dag Hammerskjöld

We are all under sentence of death, but with a sort of indefinite reprieve.
    Victor Hugo

Well, there's a remedy for all things but death, which will be sure to lay us flat one time or other.
    Miguel de Cervantes

The end of life would be much less frightening if it were not called death any more. The fear of death is the source of all religions.
    Maurice Maeterlinck

A dead atheist is someone who is all dressed up with no place to go.
    James Duffecy

Death is the only thing we haven't succeeded in completely vulgarizing.
    Aldous Huxley

Fish die belly upward, and rise to the surface. It's their way of falling.
    André Gide

Death is the only inescapable, unavoidable, sure thing. We are sentenced to die the day we're born.
    Gary Mark Gilmore

We are all dead men on leave.
    Eugene Levine

No one here gets out alive.
    Jim Morrison

We die only once: and for such a long time.
    Molière

It matters not how a man dies, but how he lives. The act of dying is not of importance, it lasts so short a time.
    Samuel Johnson

It is not death, but dying, which is terrible.
    Henry Fielding

I shot a man in Reno just to watch him die.
> Johnny Cash

No one owns life. But anyone with a frying pan owns death.
> William S. Burroughs

I am become death, shatterer of worlds.
> Robert J. Oppenheimer, quoting from the Bhagavadgita, after witnessing the world's first nuclear explosion

I don't want to achieve immortality through my work. I want to achieve it through not dying.
> Woody Allen

The first requisite for immortality is death.
> Stanislaw J. Lec

If you want your name spelled wrong, die.
> Al Blanchard

Men are convinced of your arguments, your sincerity, and the seriousness of your efforts only by your death.
> Albert Camus

'Tis after death that we measure men.
> James Barron Hope

The dead tiger leaves his pelt; man his reputation.
> Japanese proverb

Death, when it approaches, ought not to take one by surprise. It should be part of the full expectancy of life.
> Muriel Spark

Every man must do two things alone; he must do his own believing and his own dying.
> Martin Luther

He is one of those people who would be enormously improved by death.
> H.H. Munro, a.k.a. Saki

How could they tell?
> Dorothy Parker, on being told of the death of Calvin Coolidge

I have never killed a man, but I have read many obituaries with great pleasure.
> Clarence Darrow

Death should not be seen as the end – but as a very effective way to cut down expenses.
> Woody Allen

Either this man is dead or my watch has stopped.
> Groucho Marx

Death is nature's way of saying, Your table's ready.
> Robin Williams

Death twitches my ear. "Live," he says, "I am coming."
> Virgil

Since the day of my birth, my death began its walk. It is walking toward me, without hurrying.
> Jean Cocteau

Those who welcome death have only tried it from the ears up.
> Wilson Mizner

Death is more universal than life; everyone dies but not everyone lives.
> A. Sachs

Human beings make death the great boogey.
> Alan Watts

Death meant little to me. It was the last joke in a series of bad jokes.
> Charles Bukowski

If this is dying, then I don't think much of it.
> Lytton Strachey

Is death the last step? No, it is the final awakening.
> Sir Walter Scott

Life is but a journey; death is returning home.
> Chinese proverb

Death is the supreme festival on the road to freedom.
> Dietrich Bonhoeffer

To die will be an awfully big adventure.
> Sir James M. Barrie

Let's do some livin' after we die.
> Mick Jagger

It is as natural to die as to be born.
Francis Bacon

That which we call death, is but the other side of life.
Ramacharaka

Death, so called, is a thing which makes men weep, And yet a third of Life is passed in sleep.
Lord Byron

Let us endeavor so to live that when we come to die even the undertaker will be sorry.
Mark Twain

Death always comes too early or too late.
English Proverb

He whom the gods love, dies young.
Titus Maccius Plautus

The idea is to die young as late as possible.
Ashley Montague

Do not go gentle into that good night. Rage, rage against the dying of the light.
Dylan Thomas

It's not dark yet but it's gettin' there.
Bob Dylan

I'll sleep when I'm dead.
Warren Zevon

He hath lived ill that knows not how to die well.
Dr. Thomas Fuller

People living deeply have no fear of death.
Anaïs Nin

Do not fear death so much but rather the inadequate life.
Bertolt Brecht

Some people are so afraid to die that they never begin to live.
Henry Van Dyke

Our last garment is made without pockets.
Italian Proverb

Let the dead bury the dead.
      Western Koan

As men, we are all equal in the presence of death.
      Publilius Syrus

Death is a camel that lies down at every door.
      Persian Proverb

I have a piece of great and sad news to tell you: I am dead.
      Jean Cocteau

Death opens unknown doors. It is most grand to die.
      John Masefield

Them that die'll be the lucky ones.
      Long John Silver, Treasure Island

To die is different from what any supposed, and luckier.
      Walt Whitman

Dreams

Ideologies separate us. Dreams and anguish bring us together.
      Eugène Ionesco

I'll let you be in my dream if I can be in yours.
      Bob Dylan

I have had dreams and I have had nightmares, but I have conquered my nightmares because of my dreams.
      Dr. Jonas Salk

I don't use drugs, my dreams are frightening enough.
      M.C. Escher

We are such stuff
As dreams are made on;
and our little life
Is rounded with a sleep.
      William Shakespeare

For my part I know nothing with any certainty, but the sight of the stars makes me dream.
      Vincent Van Gogh

There is nothing like a dream to create the future.
> Victor Hugo

When your heart is in your dream, no request is too extreme.
> Jiminy Cricket

I have a dream.
> Martin Luther King, Jr.

So far, there is no law against dreaming.
> Winnie Mandela

Dreams are necessary to life.
> Anaïs Nin

Go confidently in the direction of your dreams. Live the life you've imagined.
> Henry David Thoreau

Dream is destiny.
> Richard Linklater

I dreamed a thousand new paths... I woke and walked my old one.
> Chinese Proverb

Those who dream by day are cognizant of many things which escape those who dream only by night.
> Edgar Allan Poe

A dreamer is one who can only find his way by moonlight, and his punishment is that he sees the dawn before the rest of the world.
> Oscar Wilde

Dreaming men are haunted men.
> Stephen Vincent Benet

Dreams are wiser than men.
> Omaha Saying

Dream as if you'll live forever. Live as if you'll die tomorrow.
> James Dean

Nothing happens unless first a dream.
> Carl Sandburg

In dreams begin responsibility.
> William Butler Yeats

Dreams have as much influence as actions.
Stéphane Mallarmé

It may be that those who do most, dream most.
Stephen Leacock

All men dream: but not equally.
T.E. Lawrence (of Arabia)

I do not know whether I was then a man dreaming I was a butterfly, or whether I am now a butterfly dreaming I am a man.
Chuang-Tzu

You know that place between asleep and awake? Where you still remember dreaming? That's where I will always think of you.
Tinkerbell

We are near awakening when we dream that we dream.
Baron Friedrich von Hardenberg

Our truest life is when we are in dreams awake.
Henry David Thoreau

If I am dreaming let me never awake, If I am awake let me never sleep.
Chinese Proverb

You have to have a dream so you can get up in the morning.
Billy Wilder

Dreams and beasts are two keys by which we find out the secret of our own nature. They are test objects.
Ralph Waldo Emerson

A dream which is not interpreted is like a letter which is not read.
The Talmud

I was not looking for my dreams to interpret my life, but rather for my life to interpret my dreams.
Susan Sontag

The inquiry into a dream is another dream.
Lord Halifax

Dreams are illustrations...from the book your soul is writing about you.
Marsha Norman

The dream is the theater where the dreamer is at once scene, actor, prompter, stage manager, author, audience and critic.
Carl Gustav Jung

We use up too much artistic effort in our dreams; in consequence our waking life is often poor.
Friedrich Nietzsche

All we see or seem is but a dream within a dream.
Edgar Allen Poe

One does not dream; one is dreamed. We undergo the dream; we are the objects.
Carl Jung

If a little dreaming is dangerous, the cure for it is not to dream less but to dream more, to dream all the time.
Marcel Proust

Your old men shall dream dreams, your young men shall see visions.
Bible: Joel 2:28

The older I become, the more I realize that dreams are something which do not fade.
Jean Cocteau

A dream is a wish your heart makes.
Cinderella

Dreams come true, without that possibility, nature would not invite us to have them.
John Updike

Saddle your dreams before you ride them.
Mary Webb

Dreaming permits each and every one of us to be quietly and safely insane every night of our lives.
William Dement

Lose your dreams and you could lose your mind.
Mick Jagger

Those who lose dreaming are lost.
Australian Aboriginal Proverb

Society often forgives the criminal; it never forgives the dreamer.
Oscar Wilde

We live, as we dream – alone.
Joseph Conrad

Dreams are the touchstones of our character.
> Henry David Thoreau

In dreams and in love there are no impossibilities.
> Janos Arnay

Dreams are true while they last, and do we not live in dreams?
> Alfred Lord Tennyson

Please, consider me a dream.
> Franz Kafka

The world is as you dream it.
> Shamanic Saying

Experience and Existentialism

Man is nothing else but what he makes of himself. Such is the first principle of existentialism.
> Jean-Paul Sartre

You must have control of the authorship of your own destiny. The pen that writes your life story must be held in your own hand.
> Irene C. Kassorla

I yam what I yam.
> Popeye

I am that I am.
> Old Testament Koan

Experience is not what happens to a man. It is what a man does with what happens to him.
> Aldous Huxley

Information's pretty thin stuff, unless mixed with experience.
> Clarence Day

Only so much do I know, as I have lived.
> Ralph Waldo Emerson

Experience is the name men give to their mistakes.
> Sonny Liston

Experience is a hard teacher, because she gives the test first, the lesson afterwards.
> Vernon S. Law

56

Good judgement comes from experience. Experience comes from bad judgement.
Jim Horning

Experience is that marvelous thing that enables you recognize a mistake when you make it again.
Franklin P. Jones

Experience increases our wisdom but doesn't reduce our follies.
Josh Billings

The only thing that experience teaches us is that experience teaches us nothing.
André Maurois

Experience is a comb that life gives you after you lose your hair.
Judith Stern

Experience is what you get when you don't get what you want.
Dan Stanford

Experience is one thing you can't get for nothing.
Oscar Wilde

Be patient and strong; for someday this pain will be useful to you.
Ovid

If I had to live my life again I'd make all the same mistakes – only sooner.
Tallulah Bankhead

Everyone is in the best seat.
John Cage

Do not look where you fell, but where you slipped.
African Proverb

A stumble may prevent a fall.
English Proverb

A fall into a ditch makes you wiser.
Chinese Proverb

Experience, which destroys innocence, also leads one back to it.
James Baldwin

The world breaks everyone, and afterward many are strong at the broken places.
Ernest Hemingway

A gem is not polished without rubbing, nor a man made perfect without trials.
Chinese Proverb

Everybody experiences far more than he understands. Yet it is experience, rather than understanding, that influences behavior.
> Marshall McLuhan

Just because something doesn't do what you planned it to do doesn't mean it's useless.
> Thomas Edison

Nothing is a waste of time if you use the experience wisely.
> Auguste Rodin

There is that difference between being kicked in the teeth and reading a description of being kicked in the teeth. Some call it existential.
> Gita Mehta

It is not the same to talk of bulls as to be in the bullring.
> Spanish Proverb

A man who carries a cat by the tail learns something he can learn in no other way.
> Mark Twain

I have an existential map. It has "You are here" written all over it.
> Steven Wright

Are you experienced?
> Jimi Hendrix

Faith

It's not dying for a faith that's hard. It's living up to it.
> William Makepeace Thackeray

Doubt isn't the opposite of faith; it is an element of faith.
> Paul Johannes Tillich

Faith and doubt both are needed, not as antagonists, but working side by side to take us around the unknown curve.
> Lillian Smith

That's the thing about faith. If you don't have it you can't understand it. And if you do, no explanation is necessary
> Major Kira Nerys

Take the first step in faith. You don't have to see the whole staircase, just take the first step.
> Martin Luther King Jr.

You don't leap a chasm in two bounds.
>   Chinese Proverb

Jump off a cliff. Build your wings on the way down.
>   Ray Bradbury

Faith embraces many truths which seem to contradict each other.
>   Blaise Pascal

Faith is, at one and the same time, absolutely necessary and altogether impossible.
>   Stanislaw Lem

Weave in faith and God will find the thread.
>   Proverb

Have faith and the way will open.
>   Quaker Saying

Faith is the refusal to panic.
>   David Martyn Lloyd-Jones

A man consists of the faith that is in him. Whatever his faith is, he is.
>   Bhagavadgita

I respect faith, but doubt is what gets you an education.
>   Wilson Mizner

Faith is the substance of things hoped for, the evidence of things not seen.
>   Bible, Hebrews 11:1

To believe only possibilities is not faith, but mere philosophy.
>   Sir Thomas Browne

You can do very little with faith, but you can do nothing without it.
>   Samuel Butler

You need a busload of faith to get by.
>   Lou Reed

Faith may be defined briefly as an illogical belief in the occurrence of the improbable.
>   H.L. Mencken

Faith is believing what you know ain't so.
>   Mark Twain

Faith consists in believing not what seems true, but what seems false
to our understanding.
    Voltaire

Faith is not contrary to reason.
    Sherwood Eddy

Faith is a higher faculty than reason.
    Henry Christopher Bailey

I believe though I do not comprehend, and I hold by faith what I cannot grasp
with the mind.
    Saint Bernard

Faith is deliberate confidence in the character of God whose ways you may not
understand at the time.
    Oswald Chambers

Conscious faith is freedom. Emotional faith is slavery. Mechanical faith
is foolishness.
    G.I. Gurdjieff

The fact that a believer is happier than a skeptic is no more to the point than the fact
that a drunken man is happier than a sober one.
    George Bernard Shaw

The believer is happy, the doubter is wise.
    Greek Proverb

The farther we go, the more the ultimate explanation recedes from us, and all
we have left is faith.
    Václav Hlavatý

Non-violence is the article of faith.
    Mahatma Gandhi

A faith that hasn't been tested can't be trusted.
    Adrian Rogers

Faith without works is dead.
    Bible, James 2:26

Faith which does not doubt is dead faith.
    Miguel de Unamuno

Certainty stunts growth.
    Gregory Mcdonald

There is more faith in an honest doubt, believe me, than in half the creeds.
    Alfred Lord Tennyson

All things are possible to him that believeth.
    Bible, Mark 9:23

When you believe in a thing, believe in it all the way.
    Walt Disney

Faith is the bird that sings when the dawn is still dark.
    Rabindranath Tagore

Belief is like love; it cannot be compelled.
    Arthur Schopenhauer

Faith is to believe what you do not see; the reward of this faith is to see what you believe.
    Saint Augustine

Some things have to be believed to be seen.
    Ralph Hodgson, on ESP

Fate and Destiny

I do not believe in a fate that falls on men however they act; but I do believe in a fate that falls on them unless they act.
    G.K. Chesterton

If Fate does not adjust itself to you, adjust yourself to Fate.
    Persian Proverb

If you can't change your fate, change your attitude.
    Chinese Proverb

Every man has his own destiny: the only imperative is to follow it, to accept it, no matter where it leads him.
    Henry Miller

Like puppets we are moved by outside strings.
    Horace

Fate leads the willing, and drags along the reluctant.
    Seneca

It is to be remarked that a good many people are born curiously unfitted for the fate waiting them on this earth.
    Joseph Conrad

Fate is not an eagle, it creeps like a rat.
    Elizabeth Bowen

Fate is nothing but the deeds committed in a prior state of existence.
    Ralph Waldo Emerson

Men are not prisoners of fate, but only prisoners of their own mind.
    Franklin D. Roosevelt

Whatever limits us, we call Fate.
    Ralph Waldo Emerson

Ask not what tomorrow may bring, but count as blessing every day that Fate allows you.
    Horace

What people commonly call fate is mostly their own stupidity.
    Arthur Schopenhauer

Lots of folks confuse bad management with destiny.
    Kim Hubbard

Destiny: A tyrant's authority for crime and a fool's excuse for failure.
    Ambrose Bierce, Devil's Dictionary

What do I know of man's destiny. I could tell you more about radishes.
    Samuel Beckett

Destiny is not a matter of chance, it is a matter of choice; it is not a thing to be waited for, it is a thing to be achieved.
    William Jennings Bryan

And when man faces destiny, destiny ends and man comes into his own.
    André Malraux

It is not in the stars to hold our destiny but in ourselves.
    William Shakespeare

Everything that happens, happens by necessity.
    Democritus

Coincidence, if traced far enough back, becomes inevitable.
    Inscription on a Hindu temple near New Delhi

Fear

Nothing in life is to be feared. It is only to be understood.
    Marie Curie

The worst fear is the fear of living.
    Theodore Roosevelt

He who fears corruption fears life.
    Saul Alinsky

The worst sorrows in life are not in its losses and misfortune, but its fears.
    A.C. Benson

Down these mean streets a man must go who is not himself mean, who is neither tarnished nor afraid.
    Raymond Chandler

Our deepest fear is not that we are inadequate. Our deepest fear is that we are powerful beyond measure. It is our Light, not our Darkness, that most frightens us.
    Nelson Mandela

What would you do if you weren't afraid.
    Dr. Spencer Johnson

Use your fear... it can take you to the place where you store your courage.
    Amelia Earhart

Do not fear mistakes; there are none.
    Miles Davis

The man who has ceased to fear has ceased to care.
    F.H. Bradley

Every man has some fear. A man with no fear belongs in a mental institution.
    Walt Michaels

Fears are educated into us, and can, if we wish, be educated out.
    Karl A. Menninger

Fear defeats more people than any other one thing in the world.
    Ralph Waldo Emerson

Fear is, I believe, a most effective tool in destroying the soul of an individual – and the soul of a people.
    Anwar el-Sadat

No passion so effectually robs the mind of all its powers of acting and reasoning as fear.
> Edmund Burke

Fear is the static that prevents me from hearing myself.
> Samuel Butler

Hatred is never anything but fear – if you feared no one, you would hate no one.
> Hugh Downs

Fear is that little darkroom where negatives are developed.
> Michael Pritchard

I have my fears but they do not have me.
> Peter Gabriel

The first and great commandment is: Don't let them scare you.
> Elmer Davis

We hope vaguely but dread precisely.
> Paul Valéry

Fear makes strangers of people who should be friends.
> Shirley McLaine

The only thing we have to fear is fear itself.
> Franklin D. Roosevelt

The only thing we have to fear on this planet is man.
> Carl Gustav Jung

Fear is a greater evil than the evil itself.
> Saint François de Sales

Fear doesn't exist anywhere except in the mind.
> Dale Carnegie

You can't underestimate the power of fear.
> Tricia Nixon

The lens of fear magnifies the size of the uncertainty.
> Charles Swindall

Fear makes the wolf bigger than he is.
> German Proverb

There is no terror in the bang, only in the anticipation of it.
> Alfred Hitchcock

There are very few monsters who warrant the fear we have of them.
André Gide

He that hath been bitten by a serpent is afraid of rope.
English proverb

We are tied to what we hate or fear.
Swami Prabhavananda

We fear things in proportion to our ignorance of them.
Titus London

Fear is the lengthened shadow of ignorance.
Arnold Glasow

What man does not understand, he fears; and what he fears, he tends to destroy.
William Butler Yeats

There is a time to take counsel of your fears, and there is a time to never listen to any fear.
George S. Patton

When we are afraid, we say that we are cautious. When others are afraid, we say that they are cowardly.
Marcel Archard

Fear is the highest fence.
Dudley Nichols

Become so wrapped up in something that you forget to be afraid.
Lady Bird Johnson

What we fear comes to pass more speedily than what we hope.
Publilius Syrus

Fear is the main source of superstition, and one of the main sources of cruelty.
Bertrand Russell

Fear is a fine spur, so is rage.
Irish Proverb

Fear can be headier than whiskey, once a man has acquired a taste for it.
Donald Downes

God is good, there is no devil but fear.
Elbert G. Hubbard

Fear not the man who fears God.
Arabian Proverb

He who is not everyday conquering some fear has not learned the secret of life
Ralph Waldo Emerson

Do the thing you fear most and the death of fear is certain.
Mark Twain

Feeling

Never apologize for showing feeling. When you do so, you apologize for the truth.
Benjamin Disraeli

Our feelings are our most genuine paths to knowledge.
Audre Lorde

Who feels it knows it.
Neville O'Reilly Livingston, a.k.a. Bunny Wailer

Feelings are everywhere – be gentle.
J. Masai

Feeling and longing are the motive forces behind all human endeavor and human creations.
Albert Einstein

Since feelings come first, who cares about the syntax of things.
e.e. cummings

I want to make people feel, to give them lessons in feeling. They can think afterwards.
John Osborne

I don't believe that life is supposed to make you feel good, or make you feel miserable either. Life is just supposed to make you feel.
Gloria Naylor

Half of our mistakes in life arise from feeling where we ought to think, and thinking where we ought to feel.
John Churton Collins

They may forget what you said, but they will never forget how you made them feel.
Carl W. Buechner

Feelings are not supposed to be logical. Dangerous is the man who has rationalized his emotions.
>   David Borenstein

Seeing's believing, but feeling's the truth.
>   Dr. Thomas Fuller

The truth of a thing is the feel of it, not the think of it.
>   Stanley Kubrick

One ounce of emotion is equal to a ton of facts.
>   John Junor

We think too much and feel too little.
>   Charlie Chaplin

Every person's feelings have a front-door and a side-door by which they may be entered.
>   Oliver Wendell Holmes, Sr.

All great discoveries are made by men whose feelings run ahead of their thinking.
>   Charles Parkhurst

Love God and trust your feelings. Be loyal to them. Don't betray them.
>   Robert C. Pollock

One must marry one's feelings to one's beliefs and ideas. That is probably the only way to achieve a measure of harmony in one's life.
>   Etty Hilsum

Never ignore a gut feeling, but never believe that it's enough.
>   Kermit the Frog

All bad poetry springs from genuine feeling.
>   Oscar Wilde

The best and most beautiful things in the world cannot be seen or even touched. They must be felt.
>   Helen Keller

Focus

If you want to hit a bird on the wing you must have all your will in focus.
Every achievement is a bird on the wing.
>   Oliver Wendell Holmes Jr.

When every physical and mental resource is focused, one's power to solve a problem multiples tremendously.
>   Norman Vincent Peale

To do two things at once is to do neither.
>   Publilius Syrus

If you chase two rabbits, both will escape.
>   Unknown

To be everywhere is to be nowhere.
>   Seneca

Do one thing at a time, and do that one thing as if your life depended on it.
>   Eugene Grace

Shoot a few scenes out of focus. I want to win the foreign film award.
>   Billy Wilder

To see what is in front of one's nose needs a constant struggle.
>   George Orwell

The first requisite of success is the ability to apply your physical and mental energies to one problem without growing weary.
>   Thomas Edison

Concentration is the secret of strengths in politics, in war, in trade, in short in all management of human affairs.
>   Ralph Waldo Emerson

Keep focused on the substantive issues. To make a decision means having to go through one door and closing all others.
>   Abraham Zaleznik

The absence of alternatives clears the mind marvelously.
>   Henry Kissinger

It is not enough to be busy; so are the ants. The question is: What are we busy about?
>   Henry David Thoreau

Be occupied, then, with what you really value and let the thief take something else.
>   Mevlâna Jalâladdîn Rumi

The human mind is not rich enough to drive many horses abreast and wants one general scheme, under which it strives to bring everything.
George Santayana

Concentrate all your thoughts on the task at hand. The sun's rays do not burn until brought to a focus.
Alexander Graham Bell

Freedom

The moment the slave resolves that he will no longer be a slave, his fetters fall. Freedom and slavery are mental states.
Mahatma Gandhi

Emancipate yourselves from mental slavery. None but ourselves can free our minds.
Bob Marley

The man who follows is a slave. The man who thinks is free.
Robert G. Ingersoll

No man can put a chain about the ankle of his fellow man without at least finding the other end of it about his own neck.
Frederick Douglass

It is dangerous to free people who prefer to be slaves.
Niccolo Machiavelli

Man is born free but is everywhere in chains.
Jean-Jacques Rousseau

If you are free, you are not predictable and you are not controllable.
June Jordan

I fear nothing, I hope nothing, I am free.
Nikos Kazantzakis

Our ultimate freedom is the right and power to decide how anybody or anything outside ourselves will affect us.
Stephen R. Covey

Freedom will cure most things.
A.S. Neill

Freedom is nothing else but a chance to be better.
Albert Camus

People demand freedom of speech as a compensation for the freedom of thought which they seldom use.
Søren Kierkegaard

The freedom of the mind is the beginning of all other freedoms.
Clinton Lee Scott

Tyrants have not yet discovered any chains that can fetter the mind.
Charles Caleb Colton

Thinking ain't illegal yet. Free your mind and your ass will follow.
George Clinton, a.k.a. Dr. Funkenstein

Freedom comes from human beings, rather than from laws and institutions.
Clarence Darrow

I had crossed the line and I was free, but there was no one to welcome me to the land of freedom. I was a stranger in a strange land.
Harriet Tubman

Man is condemned to be free; because once thrown into the world, he is responsible for everything he does.
Jean-Paul Sartre

There can be no real freedom without the freedom to fail.
Eric Hoffer

In the last analysis, our only freedom is the freedom to discipline ourselves.
Bernard M. Baruch

Knowing how to free oneself is nothing; it's being free that is hard.
André Gide

No man is free who is not a master of himself.
Epictetus

When I discover who I am, I'll be free.
Ralph Ellison

If you think you're free, there's no escape possible.
Baba Ram Dass

I don't want the cheese, I just want to get out of the trap.
Spanish Proverb

Hint: The cage is not locked.
Nova Knutson

70

The function of freedom is to free somebody else.
>> Toni Morrison

You can only be free if I am free.
>> Clarence Darrow

Your freedom and mine cannot be separated.
>> Nelson Mandela

The freedom of any society varies proportionately with the volume of its laughter.
>> Zero Mostel

What is freedom of expression? Without the freedom to offend, it ceases to exist.
>> Salmon Rushdie

Freedom is the right to tell people what they do not want to hear.
>> George Orwell

He only earns his freedom and his life who takes them every day by storm.
>> Johann Wolfgang von Goethe

Freedom means choosing your burden.
>> Hephzibah Menuhin

Freedom ain't nothing but knowing how to say what's up in your head.
>> Ralph Ellison

Freedom is the last, best hope of earth.
>> Abraham Lincoln

Freedom's just another word for nothing left to lose.
>> Kris Kristofferson

Freedom is just chaos with better lighting.
>> Alan Dean Foster

To be free is to have achieved your life.
>> Tennessee Williams

Those who profess to favor freedom, and yet depreciate agitation, are men who want rain without thunder and lightning.
>> Frederick Douglass

Freedom is not free.
>> Martin Luther King, Jr.

Nobody can give you freedom. Nobody can give you equality or justice or anything.
If you're a man, you take it.
Malcolm X

Who would be free themselves must strike the blow.
Lord Byron

There is no such thing as part freedom.
Nelson Mandela

Friendship

He who gives up a friendship for ambition burns a picture to obtain the ashes.
Arabic Proverb

If you want to find out who your friends are, get yourself a jail sentence.
Charles Bukowski

In prosperity our friends know us; in adversity we know our friends.
John Churton Collins

It is the friends you can call up at 4 a.m. that matter.
Marlene Dietrich

Friendship is a single soul dwelling in two bodies.
Aristotle

In my friend, I find a second self.
Isabel Norton

Friendship is a sheltering tree.
Samuel Taylor Coleridge

The road to a friend's house is never long.
Danish Proverb

The only way to have a friend is to be one.
Ralph Waldo Emerson

Fine friendship requires duration rather than fitful intensity.
Aristotle

You can make new friends, but you can't make old friends.
Martin Amis

The friendship which can cease has never been real.
>Saint Jerome

A friend is someone who sees through you and still enjoys the view.
>Wilma Askinas

A friend is one who knows you and loves you just the same.
>Elbert G. Hubbard

Who seeks a faultless friend remains friendless.
>Turkish Proverb

Only your real friends will tell you when your face is dirty.
>Sicilian Proverb

A true friend stabs you in the front.
>Oscar Wilde

Keep your friends close, but your enemies closer.
>Niccolo Machiavelli

May God defend me from my friends; I can defend myself from my enemies.
>Voltaire

Choose your friends carefully. Your enemies will choose you.
>Yassir Arafat

You can't eat your friends and have them too.
>Budd Schulberg

I can't be your friend and your flatterer too.
>Proverb

A friend's eye is a good mirror.
>Irish Proverb

Don't speak badly of my friends; I am capable of doing that just as well as you.
>Sacha Guitry

That man travels the longest journey that undertakes it in search of a sincere friend.
>Ali Ibn-Abi-Talib

The worst solitude is to be destitute of sincere friendship.
>Francis Bacon

The difficulty is not so great to die for a friend, as to find a friend worth dying for.
>Homer

You cannot be friends upon any other terms than upon the terms of equality.
    Woodrow Wilson

Friendship is like money, easier made than kept.
    Samuel Butler

True friendship is like sound health, the value of it is seldom known until it be lost.
    Charles Caleb Colton

A man's friendships are one of the best measures of his worth.
    Charles Darwin

The finest kind of friendship is between people who expect a great deal of each other but never ask it.
    Sylvia Bremer

Friendship is a furrow in the sand.
    Tongan Proverb

Love demands infinitely less than friendship.
    George Jean Nathan

Friendship without self-interest is one of the rare and beautiful things of life.
    James Byrnes

He who hath many friends hath none.
    Aristotle

Hold a true friend with both your hands.
    Nigerian Proverb

Tell me what company you keep, and I'll tell you who you are.
    Miguel de Cervantes

Each friend represents a world in us, a world possibly not born until they arrive, and it is only by this meeting that this new world is born.
    Anaïs Nin

How rare and wonderful is that flash of a moment when we realize we have discovered a friend.
    William Rotsler

Do not protect yourself by a fence, but rather by your friends.
    Czech Proverb

A real friend is one who walks in when the rest of the world walks out.
    Walter Winchell

You can make more friends in two months by becoming more interested in other people than you can in two years by trying to get people interested in you.
> Dale Carnegie

The real test of friendship is: can you literally do nothing with the other person? Can you enjoy those moments of life that are utterly simple?
> Eugene Kennedy

It is one of the blessings of old friends that you can afford to be stupid with them.
> Ralph Waldo Emerson

The language of friendship is not words but meanings.
> Henry David Thoreau

A friend may be the masterpiece of nature.
> Ralph Waldo Emerson

The Future

Telling the future by looking at the past assumes that conditions remain constant. This is like driving a car by looking in the rear view mirror.
> Herb Brody

Study the past if you would divine the future.
> Confucius

In this great future you can't forget your past.
> Bob Marley

The future is only the past again, entered through another gate.
> Arthur Wing Pinero

I don't think of the future. It will come soon enough.
> Albert Einstein

The best thing about the future is that it only comes one day at a time.
> Dean Acheson

The days run away like horses over the hill.
> Charles Bukowski

The future has a way of arriving unannounced.
> George F. Will

We should all be concerned about the future because we will have to spend the rest of our lives there.
  Charles F. Kettering

We steal if we touch tomorrow. It is God's.
  Henry Ward Beecher

Prediction is extremely difficult. Especially about the future.
  Niels Bohr

The future ain't what it used to be.
  Yogi Berra

One should never place confidence in the future – it doesn't deserve it.
  Paul Chamson

People live for the morrow, because the day-after-to-morrow is doubtful.
  Friedrich Nietzsche

The future is called "perhaps," which is the only possible thing to call the future.
  Tennessee Williams

Just remember – when you think all is lost, the future remains.
  Robert Goddard

As long as we have some definite idea about or some hope in the future, we cannot really be serious with the moment that exists right now.
  Shunryu Suzuki Roshi

I don't try to describe the future. I try to prevent it.
  Ray Bradbury

I have seen the future and it doesn't work.
  Robert Fulford

The future is a mirror with no glass.
  Xavier Forneret

Real generosity toward the future lies in giving all to the present.
  Albert Camus

The future is like heaven – everyone exalts it, but no one wants to go there now.
  James Baldwin

The future is much like the present, only longer.
  Don Quisenberry

There is always one moment in childhood when the door opens and lets the future in.
Graham Greene

The future belongs to those who believe in the beauty of their dreams.
Eleanor Roosevelt

I like the dreams of the future better than the history of the past.
Thomas Jefferson

No matter what a man's past may have been, his future is spotless.
John R. Rice

The future starts today, not tomorrow.
Pope John Paul II

The future belongs to those who prepare for it today.
Malcolm X

The future is today.
William Osler

The future is already here it is just unevenly distributed.
William Gibson

This is my prediction for the future – whatever hasn't happened will happen
and no one will be safe from it.
J.B.S. Haldane

The only certain thing about the future is that it will surprise even those who have
seen furthest into it
E.J. Hobsbawn

The future is a time when the entire past will be known.
Gabriel Laub

Future, n. That period of time in which our affairs prosper, our friends are true
and our happiness is assured.
Ambrose Bierce, The Devil's Dictionary

I have long considered it one of God's greatest mercies that the future is hidden from
us. If it were not, life would surely be unbearable.
Eugene Forsey

It is bad enough to know the past; it would be intolerable to know the future.
W. Somerset Maugham

It is a mistake to look too far ahead. Only one link in the chain of destiny can be handled at a time.
    Winston Churchill

If you want a picture of the future, imagine a boot stamping on the human face – forever.
    George Orwell

As for the Future, your task is not to foresee, but to enable it.
    Antoine de Saint-Exupéry

Remember this, and also be reminded of its truth – the future is not in the hands of fate, but in ourselves.
    Jean Jules Jusserand

The best way to predict the future is to invent it.
    Alan Kay

Generosity

The only gift is a portion of yourself.
    Ralph Waldo Emerson

All you are unable to give possesses you.
    André Gide

If you give what you do not need, it isn't giving.
    Mother Teresa

The more one gives to others, the more he has for his own.
    Lao-Tzu

No one is so generous as he who has nothing to give.
    French Proverb

For it is in giving that we receive.
    Saint Francis of Assisi

I have found that among its other benefits, giving liberates the soul of the giver.
    Maya Angelou

The manner of giving is worth more than the gift.
    Pierre Corneille

Generosity lies less in giving much than in giving at the right moment.
    Jean de La Bruyère

No man can become rich without himself enriching others.
Andrew Carnegie

Not he who has much is rich, but he who gives much.
Erich Fromm

Think of giving not as a duty but as a privilege.
John D. Rockefeller Jr.

To give without any reward, or any notice, has a special quality of its own.
Anne Morrow Lindbergh

Give, expecting nothing thereof.
Saint Thomas Aquinas

To generous souls every task is noble.
Euripides

To give quickly is a great virtue.
Hindu Proverb

He who gives to me teaches me to give.
Danish Proverb

Nothing that you have not given away will ever be really yours.
C.S. Lewis

Genius

Everyone is a genius at least once a year. The real geniuses simply have their bright ideas closer together.
Georg Christoph Lichtenberg

Everyone is born with genius, but most people only keep it a few minutes.
Edgard Varèse

Geniuses do not think more than other people. They think less.
Len Cool

Genius makes its observations in short-hand; talent writes them out at length.
Christian Nevell Bovee

Talent does what it can; genius does what it must.
Edward George Bulwer-Lytton

I probably have genius. But no talent.
Francis Ford Coppola, attributed

Genius points the way, talent takes it.
Maria von Ebner-Eschenbach

Genius, like electricity, is not to be analyzed.
Jean Cocteau

One of the strongest characteristics of genius is the power of lighting its own fire.
John W. Foster

Genius may have its limitations, but stupidity is not thus handicapped.
Elbert G. Hubbard

We know that the nature of genius is to provide idiots with ideas twenty years later.
Louis Aragon

Since when was genius found respectable?
Elizabeth Barrett Browning

Genius is eternal patience.
Michelangelo

Genius is nothing but a power of sustained attention.
William James

If you knew how much work went into it, you wouldn't call it genius.
Michelangelo

Genius is the capacity to make all possible mistakes in the least amount of time.
Niels Bohr

True genius resides in the capacity for evaluation of uncertain, hazardous, and conflicting information.
Winston Churchill

No great genius has ever been without some madness.
Aristotle

Whom the gods wish to destroy they first call promising.
Cyril Connolly

A man of genius has been seldom ruined but by himself.
Samuel Johnson

I don't want to be a genius, I have enough problems just trying to be a man.
Albert Camus

The definition of genius is that it acts unconsciously; and those who have produced immortal works have done so without knowing how or why.
> William Hazlitt

Genius is the ability to put into effect what is in your mind.
> F. Scott Fitzgerald

Neither a lofty degree of intelligence nor imagination nor both together go to the making of genius. Love, love, love, that is the soul of genius.
> Wolfgang Amadeus Mozart

First and last, what is demanded of genius is love of truth.
> Johann Wolfgang von Goethe

Genius not only diagnoses the situation but supplies the answer.
> Robert Graves

Genius means nothing more than the faculty of perceiving in an unhabitual way.
> William James

We define genius as the capacity for productive reaction against one's training.
> Bernard Berenson

It is the essence of genius to make use of the simplest idea.
> Charles Péguy

To see things in the seed, that is genius.
> Lao-Tzu

I believe that instinct is what makes a genius a genius.
> Bob Dylan

The thinking of a genius does not proceed logically. It leaps with great ellipses. It pulls knowledge from God knows where.
> Dorothy Thompson

You cannot create genius. All you can do is nurture it.
> Ninette de Valois

If you can't be a genius, imitate the daring.
> Eudora Welty

When a true genius appears in the world, you may know him by this sign that the dunces are all in confederacy against him.
> Jonathan Swift

The public is wonderfully tolerant. It forgives everything except genius.
> Oscar Wilde

God

God, it seems, is a verb, not a noun, proper or improper.
R. Buckminster Fuller

Why is it when we talk to God we're praying – but when God talks to us, we're schizophrenic?
Lily Tomlin

I believe more and more that God must not be judged on this earth. It is one of his sketches that has turned out badly.
Vincent Van Gogh

God does not play dice with the universe.
Albert Einstein

Not only does God play dice, but he sometimes throws them where they cannot be seen.
Stephen Hawking

God is not dead but alive and well and working on a much less ambitious project.
Graffito

They say that God is everywhere, and yet we always think of Him as somewhat of a recluse.
Emily Dickinson

Where does one find God? In the mountains, the solitary wooded valleys, strange islands... silent music.
Saint John of the Cross

Man is certainly stark mad. He cannot make a worm, and yet he will be making gods by the dozens.
Michel de Montaigne

God is in me or else is not at all.
Wallace Stevens

What sort of God would it be who only pushed from without?
Johann Wolfgang von Goethe

God is the indwelling and not the transient cause of all things.
Baruch de Spinoza

God is a comedian playing to an audience too afraid to laugh.
Voltaire

What men usually ask for when they pray to God is, that two and two may not make four.
>Russian Proverb

God is for men and religion for women.
>Joseph Conrad

The nature of God is a circle of which the center is everywhere and the circumference is nowhere.
>Empedocles

Never place a period where God has placed a comma.
>Gracie Allen

There is no God but God.
>The Koran

We do not know what God is. God himself doesn't know what He is because He is not anything. Literally God is not, because He transcends being.
>John Scotus Erigena

If God did not exist, he would have to be invented.
>Voltaire

He was a wise man who invented God.
>Plato

It may be that our role on this planet is not to worship God, but to create him.
>Arthur C. Clarke

If God created us in his own image, we have more than reciprocated.
>Voltaire

I cannot believe in a God who wants to be praised all the time.
>Friedrich Nietzsche

A God who let us prove his existence would be an idol.
>Dietrich Bonhoeffer

I could prove God statistically.
>George Gallup

A comprehended God is no God.
>Saint John Chrysostom

That God has managed to survive the inanities of the religions that do Him homage is truly a miraculous proof of His existence.
>Ben Hecht

It is the final proof of God's omnipotence that He need not exist in order to save us.
  Peter DeVries

God is operationally, somebody who's beginning to resemble not a ruler,
but the last fading smile of a cosmic Cheshire cat.
  Sir Julian Huxley

The eye with which I see God is the same eye with which God sees me.
  Meister Eckhart

God is the name we give our conscience.
  Nader Shureih

God is subtle, but he is not malicious.
  Albert Einstein

A God all mercy is a God unjust.
  Edward Young

God will forgive me; it is his trade.
  Heinrich Heine, reportedly said on his deathbed

When the gods wish to punish us, they answer our prayers.
  Oscar Wilde

God is a concept by which we measure our pain.
  John Lennon

God, that dumping ground of our dreams.
  Jean Rostand

Not only is there no God, but try getting a plumber on weekends.
  Woody Allen

God always has another custard pie up his sleeve.
  Lynn Redgrave

The best way to know God is to love many things.
  Vincent Van Gogh

God is love.
  Bible, 1 John 4:8

Before you can find God you must lose yourself.
  Baal Shem Tov

Happiness

The purpose of our lives is to be happy.
> Tenzin Gyatso, 14th Dalai Lama

We all live with the objective of being happy; our lives are all different
and yet the same.
> Anne Frank

Men can only be happy when they do not assume that the object of life is happiness.
> George Orwell

To be happy, you must first make others happy.
> Swedish Proverb

Happiness is a how, not a what; a talent, not an object
> Hermann Hesse

Happiness is not a goal, it's a by-product.
> Eleanor Roosevelt

If you are not happy here and now, you never will be.
> Taisen Deshimaru

It is not easy to find happiness in ourselves, and it is not possible to find it elsewhere.
> Agnes Repplier

The foolish man seeks happiness in the distance, the wise grows it under his feet.
> James Oppenheim

The first recipe for happiness is: Avoid too lengthy meditations on the past.
> André Maurois

Happiness isn't something you experience; it's something you remember.
> Oscar Levant

Happiness is nothing more than good health and a bad memory.
> Albert Schweitzer

It's never too late for a happy childhood.
> Tom Robbins

A happy childhood is poor preparation for human contacts.
> Colette

Happiness is like the pox. Catch it too soon and it ruins your constitution.
> Anonymous

All the unhappiness of man stems from one thing only; that he is incapable of staying quietly in his room.
    Blaise Pascal

Happiness is having a scratch for every itch.
    Ogden Nash

There is only one happiness in this life, to love and be loved.
    George Sand

All Happiness is innocence.
    Marguerite Yourcenar

It is not how much we have, but how much we enjoy, that makes happiness.
    Charles Spurgeon

The essence of philosophy is that a man should so live that his happiness shall depend as little as possible on external things.
    Epictetus

It is very simple to be happy, but it is very difficult to be simple.
    Rabindranath Tagore

Don't Worry, Be Happy.
    Meher Baba

Happiness makes up in height for what it lacks in length.
    Robert Frost

I'm sure the way to be happy is to live well beyond your means!
    Ruth Gordon

Most people are about as happy as they make up their mind to be.
    Abraham Lincoln

He is happy that knoweth not himself to be otherwise.
    Dr. Thomas Fuller

We are never so happy or so unhappy as we imagine.
    François duc de la Rochefoucauld

Happiness depends upon ourselves.
    Aristotle

Remember, happiness doesn't depend upon who you are or what you have, it depends solely upon what you think.
    Dale Carnegie

Ask yourself whether you are happy, and you cease to be so.
    John Stuart Mill

To describe happiness is to diminish it.
    Stendhal

Happiness can be possessed only as long as it is unseen.
    Hermann Hesse

The pursuit of happiness is a most ridiculous phrase: if you pursue happiness you'll never find it.
    C.P. Snow

If only we'd stop trying to be happy we could have a pretty good time.
    Edith Wharton

He's simply got the instinct for being unhappy highly developed.
    H.H. Munro, a.k.a. Saki

Happiness is as a butterfly which, when pursued, is always beyond our grasp, but which if you will sit down quietly, may alight upon you.
    Nathaniel Hawthorne

Happiness is a branch on which you can land but not make your nest
    Comtesse Diane

The greatest happiness you can have is knowing that you do not necessarily require happiness.
    William Saroyan

The world is full of people looking for spectacular happiness while they snub contentment.
    Doug Larson

A great obstacle to happiness is to expect too much happiness.
    Bernard le Bovier de Fontenelle

I accept life unconditionally. Most people ask for happiness on condition. Happiness can only be felt if you don't set any condition.
    Arthur Rubenstein

Happiness is a function of accepting what is.
    Werner Erhard

The secret of happiness is not in doing what one likes, but in liking what one does.
    Sir James M. Barrie

Be happy while you're living, for you're a long time dead.
    Scottish Proverb

The chief happiness (for a man) is to be what he is.
    Desiderius Erasmus

Happiness is when what you think, what you say, and what you do are in harmony.
    Mahatma Gandhi

The only ones among you who will be really happy are those who have sought
and found how to serve.
    Albert Schweitzer

That is happiness: to be dissolved into something complete and great.
    Willa Cather

Every happy life cannot be without a measure of darkness, and the word "happiness"
would loose its meaning if it were not balanced by sadness.
    Carl Gustav Jung

Happiness is not a horse; you cannot harness it.
    Russian Proverb

All you need for happiness is a good gun, a good horse, and a good wife.
    Daniel Boone

A table, a chair, a bowl of fruit and a violin; what else does a man need to be happy?
    Albert Einstein

A lifetime of happiness! No man alive could bear it; it would be hell on earth.
    George Bernard Shaw

Some cause happiness wherever they go; others, whenever they go.
    Oscar Wilde

Our happiness hinges not on good luck; it hinges on peace of heart.
    David Steindl-Rast

The secret of a happy life is to accept change gracefully.
    James Stewart

When one door of happiness closes, another opens; but often we look so long
at the closed door that we do not see the one which has been opened for us.
    Helen Keller

Happiness sneaks through a door you didn't know that you left open.
    John Barrymore

What do you take me for, an idiot?
> Charles de Gaulle, when a journalist asked him if he was happy

No man is happy without a delusion of some kind. Delusions are as necessary to our happiness as realities.
> Christian Nestell Bovee

Many people are extremely happy, but are absolutely worthless to society.
> Charles Gow

Be happy, but never satisfied.
> Bruce Lee

To be without some of the things you want is an indispensable part of happiness.
> Bertrand Russell

Happiness in intelligent people is the rarest thing I know.
> Ernest Hemingway

Most people would rather be certain they're miserable, than risk being happy.
> Robert Anthony

The certainty of misery is better than the misery of uncertainty.
> Walt Kelly

Be happy. It is a way of being wise.
> Colette

The grand essentials of happiness are: something to do, something to love, and something to hope for.
> Allan K. Chalmers

Health

My health is good; it's my age that's bad.
> Roy Acuff, at 83

If I'd known I was gonna live this long, I'd have taken better care of myself.
> Eubie Blake, at 100

Go away... I'm alright.
> H.G. Wells, last words

If you wish to keep as well as possible, the less you think about your health the better.
> Oliver Wendell Holmes

Quit worrying about your health. It'll go away.
    Robert Orben

Attention to health is life's greatest hindrance.
    Plato

Invalids live the longest.
    Japanese proverb

To wish to be well is part of becoming well.
    Seneca

It is no measure of health to be well adjusted to a profoundly sick society.
    Jiddu Krishnamurti

To keep the body in good health is a duty otherwise we shall not be able to keep our mind strong and clear.
    Buddha

The human body is the best picture of the human soul.
    Ludwig Wittgenstein

The body never lies.
    Martha Graham

The first wealth is health.
    Ralph Waldo Emerson

He who has health, has hope; and he who has hope, has everything.
    Arabian Proverb

Be careful about reading health books. You may die of a misprint.
    Mark Twain

An imaginary ailment is worse than a disease.
    Hanan J. Ayalti

He who conceals his disease cannot expect to be cured.
    Ethiopian Proverb

The art of medicine consists of amusing the patient while nature cures the disease.
    Voltaire

A healthy person is one who has not been adequately researched.
    Mohan Singh

I am dying with the help of too many physicians.
    Alexander the Great, on his deathbed

90

Health nuts are going to feel stupid someday, lying in hospitals dying of nothing.
        Redd Foxx

The only way to keep your health is to eat what you don't want, drink what you don't like, and do what you'd rather not.
        Mark Twain

I believe every human has a finite number of heartbeats. I don't intend to waste any of mine running around doing exercises.
        Neil Armstrong

Use your health, even to the point of wearing it out...spend all you have before you die; and do not outlive yourself.
        George Bernard Shaw

Health is merely the slowest way someone can die.
        Unknown

A hospital is no place to be sick.
        Samuel Goldwyn

Never go to a doctor whose office plants have died.
        Erma Bombeck

Heart

It is only with the heart that one can see clearly; what is essential is invisible to the eye.
        Antoine de Saint-Exupéry

Your vision will become clear only when you look into your heart. Who looks outside, dreams. Who looks inside, awakens.
        Carl Gustav Jung

When the heart is right, "for" and "against" are forgotten.
        Thomas Merton

If I create from the heart, nearly everything works; if from the head, almost nothing.
        Marc Chagall

The best composers have a cool head and hot heart.
        Antonio Vivaldi

Let my heart be wise. It is the gods' best gift.
        Euripides

The heart is wiser than the intellect.
J.G. Holland

In the small matters trust the mind, in the large ones the heart.
Sigmund Freud

When your heart speaks, take good notes.
Judith Campbell

When the heart speaks, the mind finds it indecent to object.
Milan Kundera

There is no instinct like that of the heart.
Lord Byron

Listen and attend with the ear of your heart.
Saint Benedict

I keep a close watch on this heart of mine.
Johnny Cash

As he thinketh in his heart, so is he.
Bible, Proverbs 23:7

One learns people through the heart, not the eyes or the intellect.
Mark Twain

Who is narrow of vision cannot be big of heart.
Chinese Proverb

In a full heart there is room for everything, and in an empty heart there is room for nothing.
Antonio Porchia

The worst prison is a closed heart.
Pope John Paul II

My heart is pure as the driven slush.
Tallulah Bankhead

This heart is useless. I must have another one.
The Bride of Frankenstein

I had set my heart on shadows.
Saint Augustine

I walk a lonely street.
Anonymous suicide note; inspiration for "Heartbreak Hotel" lyric

Don't be reckless with other peoples' hearts, and don't put up with people
who are reckless with yours.
        Kurt Vonnegut

It is better to break one's heart than to do nothing with it.
        Margaret Kennedy

There's nothing more whole than a broken heart.
        Yiddish Proverb

If I keep a green bough in my heart, the singing bird will come.
        Chinese Proverb

There is no charm equal to tenderness of the heart.
        Jane Austen

Your work is to discover your world and then with all your heart give yourself to it.
        Buddha

A light heart lives long.
        William Shakespeare

Blessed are the pure in heart for they alone shall see God.
        Bible, Matthew 5:8

Nowhere are there more hiding places than in the heart.
        German Proverb

There is no end of things in the heart.
        Ezra Pound

Nobody has ever measured, not even poets, how much the heart can hold.
        Zelda Fitzgerald

There is as much in that little space within the heart as there is in the whole universe.
        Chhandogya Upanishad

Always there remain portions of our heart into which no one is able to enter,
invite them as we may.
        Mary Dixon Thayer

The heart has its reasons which reason knows nothing of.
        Blaise Pascal

Not all those who know their minds know their hearts as well.
        Francois, Duc De La Rochefoucauld

Throw your heart over the fence and the rest will follow.
Norman Vincent Peale

In spite of everything, I still believe that people are really good at heart.
Anne Frank

The only lasting beauty is the beauty of the heart.
Mevlâna Jalâladdîn Rumi

There are many paths to enlightenment. Be sure to take one with a heart.
Lao-Tzu

Wheresoever you go, go with all your heart.
Confucius

Heaven

Heaven is under our feet as well as over our heads.
Henry David Thoreau

Heaven will be inherited by every man who has heaven in his soul.
Henry Ward Beecher

The kingdom of heaven is within you.
Jesus Christ

Heaven means to be one with God.
Confucius

What they do in heaven we are ignorant of; what they do not do we are told expressly.
Jonathan Swift

Do not ask God for the way to heaven; He will show you the hardest one.
Stanislaw J. Lec

You grow to heaven. You don't go to heaven.
Edgar Cayce

The best way to get to heaven is to take it with you.
Henry Drummond

A man's reach should exceed his grasp or else what's heaven for.
Robert Browning

When I die, I hope to go to Heaven, whatever the Hell that is.
> Ayn Rand

Everybody wants to go to heaven, but nobody wants to die.
> Joe Louis

What a pity that the only way to heaven is in a hearse.
> Stanislaw J. Lec

May you get to Heaven a half hour before the Devil knows you're dead.
> Irish Proverb

This world cannot explain its own difficulties without the assistance of another.
> Charles Caleb Colton

Probably no invention came more easily to man than Heaven.
> Georg Christoph Lichtenberg

Heaven is a place where nothing ever happens.
> David Byrne

If you are not allowed to laugh in heaven, I don't want to go there.
> Martin Luther

In heaven, all the interesting people are missing.
> Friedrich Nietzsche

Go to Heaven for the climate, Hell for the company.
> Mark Twain

The devil does a nice business for such a lousy location.
> Dan Bennett

The heaven of each is but what each desires.
> Thomas Moore

I shall hear in Heaven.
> Ludwig van Beethoven, referring to his deafness

Heaven, once attained, will work backwards and turn even that agony into a glory.
> C.S. Lewis

The mind is its own place, and in itself can make a heaven of hell, a hell of heaven.
> John Milton

Heaven is equally distant everywhere.
> Petronius

As much of heaven is visible as we have eyes to see.
    William Winter

We have our brush and colors – paint Paradise and in we go.
    Nikos Kazantzakis

Hell

I love hell. I can't wait to get back.
    Malcolm Lowry

I'm dragging the audience to hell with me.
    Jerry Lee Lewis

To appreciate heaven well, it's good for a person to have some fifteen minutes of hell.
    Will Carleton

Hell is a half-filled auditorium.
    Robert Frost

Hell is truth seen too late.
    Georg Wilhelm Friedrich Hegel

The road to hell is paved with good intentions.
    Karl Marx

Hell is not as bad as the road to it.
    Yiddish proverb

If there is not Hell, a good many preachers are obtaining money under false pretenses.
    William Sunday

Believing in Hell must distort every judgement on this life.
    Cyril Connolly

I hold it to be the inalienable right of anybody to go to hell in his own way.
    Robert Frost

I got what I have now through knowing the right time to tell terrible people when to go to hell.
    Leslie Caron

You need a man to go to hell with.
    Tuesday Weld

To work hard, to live hard, to die hard, and then to go to hell after all would be too damned hard.
Carl Sandburg

I am completely convinced that hell does not exist except in the minds of pious sadists.
Isaac Asimov

Hell is the place where nothing connects.
T.S. Eliot

Hell has three gates: lust, anger, and greed.
Bhagavadgita

I believe that I am in hell, therefore I am there.
Arthur Rimbaud

If you're going through hell, keep going.
Winston Churchill

Maybe this world is another planet's hell.
Aldous Huxley

One can dream of something more terrible than a hell where one suffers; it's a hell where one would get bored.
Victor Hugo

Each of us bears his own hell.
Virgil

Hell is other people.
Jean-Paul Sartre

Hope

Hope is a good breakfast, but it is a bad supper.
Francis Bacon

Hope is generally a wrong guide, though it is very good company by the way.
Lord Halifax

Hope is a waking dream.
Aristotle

If it were not for hopes, the heart would break.
Dr. Thomas Fuller

We must accept finite disappointment, but never lose infinite hope.
>> Martin Luther King Jr.

Hope is not the conviction that something will turn out well, but the certainty that something makes sense, regardless of how it turns out.
>> Vaclav Havel

A person, who no matter how desperate the situation, gives others hope, is a true leader.
>> Daisaku Ikeda

Hope has two beautiful daughters: anger at the way things are, and the courage to see that they do not stay that way.
>> Saint Augustine

Hope springs eternal.
>> Proverb

Hope is a risk that must be run.
>> Georges Bernanos

The very least you can do in your life is to figure out what you hope for. And the most you can do is live inside that hope.
>> Barbara Kingsolver

Hope, deceitful as it is, serves at least to lead us to the end of our lives by an agreeable route.
>> François Duc de La Rochefoucauld

Hope is some extraordinary spiritual grace that God gives us to control our fears, not to oust them.
>> Vincent McNabb

Hope deceives more men than cunning does.
>> Marquis de Vauvenargues

Hope is the poor man's bread.
>> Thales of Miletus

Hope is the thing with feathers. That perches in the soul. And sings the tune without the words. And never stops at all.
>> Emily Dickinson

Hope is faith holding out its hand in the dark.
>> George Iles

Hope is the feeling you have that the feeling you have isn't permanent.
>> Jean Kerr

Hope is independent of the apparatus of logic.
    Norman Cousins

He fishes on who catches one.
    French Proverb

The miserable have no other medicine. But only hope.
    William Shakespeare

There is no medicine like hope, no incentive so great, and no tonic so powerful as expectation of something better tomorrow.
    Orison Swett Marden

Blessed is the man who expects nothing.
    Alexander Pope

Hope is a very unruly emotion.
    Gloria Steinem

Everything that is done in the world is done by hope.
    Martin Luther

When you say a situation or a person is hopeless, you are slamming the door in the face of God.
    Charles L. Allen

Abandon hope, all ye who enter here.
    Dante Alighieri, sign at the gates of Hell

Hope never abandons you, you abandon it.
    George Weinberg

Where there's life there's hope.
    Theocritus

Humanity

Remember your humanity and forget the rest.
    Albert Einstein

Our humanity were a poor thing were it not for the divinity which stirs within us.
    Francis Bacon

You cannot change humanity, you can only know it.
    Anonymous

I love mankind; it's people I can't stand.
Charles Schulz

It is easier to love humanity than to love your neighbor.
Eric Hoffer

I don't hate people. I just feel better when they're not around.
Charles Bukowski

Being human is difficult. Becoming human is a lifelong process. To be truly human is a gift.
Abraham Heschel

I believe I have no prejudices whatsoever. All I need to know is that a man is a member of the human race. That's bad enough for me.
Mark Twain

How embarrassing to be human.
Kurt Vonnegut

I am part of all that I have met.
Lord Alfred Tennyson

I am he as you are he as you are me and we are all together.
John Lennon

The fundamental delusion of humanity is to suppose that I am here and you are out there.
Yasutani Roshi

Only that in you which is me can hear what I'm saying.
Baba Ram Dass

It is not our purpose to become each other; it is to recognize each other, to learn to see the other and honor him for what he is.
Hermann Hesse

If you want to lift yourself up, lift up someone else.
Booker T. Washington

There are no passengers on spaceship earth. We are all crew.
Marshall McLuhan

No man is an island, entire of itself; every man is a piece of continent, a part of the main.
John Donne

An individual has not started living until he can rise above the narrow confines of his individualistic concerns to the broader concerns of all humanity.
>Martin Luther King, Jr.

Our humanity rests upon a series of learned behaviors, woven together into patterns that are infinitely fragile and never directly inherited.
>Margaret Mead

Be gentle to all and stern with yourself.
>Saint Teresa of Avila

Humanity has advanced, when it has advanced, not because it has been sober, responsible, and cautious, but because it has been playful, rebellious, and immature.
>Tom Robbins

Human Relations

You can discover more about a person in an hour of play than in a year of conversation.
>Plato

The meeting of two personalities is like the contact of two chemical substances: if there is any reaction, both are transformed.
>Carl Gustav Jung

We are here to help each other get through this thing, whatever it is.
>Dr. Mark Vonnegut

Treat people as if they were what they ought to be and you will help them become what they are capable of becoming.
>Johann Wolfgang von Goethe

Never look down on anybody unless you're helping him up.
>Jesse Jackson

Never go to bed with a woman who has more troubles than you.
>Ross MacDonald

Women may be able to fake orgasms, but men can fake whole relationships.
>James Shubert

The most important thing is sincerity. If you can fake that, you've got it made.
>George Burns

When you meet a swordsman, draw your sword; do not recite poetry to one who is not a poet.
    Ch'an Buddhist text

If you hate a person, you hate something in him that is part of yourself. What isn't part of ourselves doesn't disturb us.
    Hermann Hesse

Everything that irritates us about others can lead us to an understanding of ourselves.
    Carl Gustav Jung

I've always been interested in people, but I've never liked them.
    W. Somerset Maugham

Forgive your enemies but never forget their names.
    John F. Kennedy

Let there be spaces in your togetherness.
    Kahlil Gibran

What the public reproaches you for – cultivate. It's you.
    Jean Cocteau

When we ask advice, we are usually looking for an accomplice.
    Marquis de LaGrange

Advice is what we ask for when we already know the answer but wish we didn't.
    Erica Jong

Give every man thy ear, but few thy voice.
    William Shakespeare

Never keep up with the Joneses. Drag them down to your level.
    Quentin Crisp

I loathe people who keep dogs. They are cowards who haven't got the guts to bite people themselves.
    August Strindberg

My idea of an agreeable person is a person who agrees with me.
    Benjamin Disraeli

I have never in my life learned anything from any man who agreed with me.
    Dudley F. Malone

There is nothing more exhilarating than to be shot at without result.
    Winston Churchill

You begin saving the world by saving one person at a time; all else is grandiose romanticism or politics.
Charles Bukowski

To the world you may be one person but to one person you may be the world.
Mahatma Gandhi

Ideas

All the good ideas I ever had came to me while I was milking a cow.
Grant Wood

No one has ever had an idea in a dress suit.
Sir Frederick G. Banting

An idea is salvation by imagination.
Frank Lloyd Wright

All great ideas are dangerous.
Oscar Wilde

Nothing is more dangerous than an idea, when you only have one.
Alain Chartier

He had only one idea, and that was wrong.
Benjamin Disraeli

I had a monumental idea this morning, but I didn't like it.
Samuel Goldwyn

Lack of money is no obstacle. Lack of an idea is an obstacle.
Ken Hakuta

What matters is not the idea a man holds, but the depth at which he holds it.
Ezra Pound

An idea isn't responsible for the people who believe in it.
Don Marquis

If you are in love with an idea, you are no judge of its beauty or value.
Wendell Castle

To love an idea is to love a little more than one should.
Jean Rostand

To die for an idea is to set a rather high price on conjecture.
Anatole France

You can't shoot an idea.
Thomas E. Dewey

A man may die, nations may rise and fall, but an idea lives on. Ideas have endurance without death.
John F. Kennedy

We are governed not by armies, but by ideas.
Mona Caird

There is one thing stronger than all the armies in the world, and that is an idea whose time has come.
Victor Hugo

Ideas move fast when their time comes.
Carolyn Heilbrun

I can't understand why people are afraid of new ideas. I'm afraid of the old ones.
John Cage

An idea is a point of departure and no more. As soon as you elaborate it, it becomes transformed by thought.
Pablo Picasso

It doesn't matter how new an idea is: what matters is how new it becomes.
Elias Canetti

A mediocre idea that generates enthusiasm will go further than a great idea that inspires no one.
Mary Kaye Ash

If an idea, I reasoned, were really a valuable one, there must be some way of realizing it.
Elizabeth Blackwell

Out beyond ideas of wrongdoing and rightdoing, there is a field. Meet me there.
Mevlâna Jalâladdîn Rumi

Man's mind, once stretched by a new idea, never regains its original dimension.
Oliver Wendell Holmes

The only sure weapon against bad ideas is better ideas.
Whitney Griswold

The best way to have a good idea is to have a lot of ideas.
    Linus Pauling

Good ideas may fail but are not lost.
    Publilius Syrus

If at first the idea is not absurd, then there is no hope for it.
    Albert Einstein

Don't worry about people stealing your ideas. If your ideas are any good, you'll have to ram them down people's throats.
    Howard Aiken

A person with a new idea is a crank until the idea succeeds.
    Mark Twain

The ideas dictate everything, you have to be true to that or you're dead.
    David Lynch

Great ideas need landing gear as well as wings.
    C.O. Jackson

Harold, like the rest of us, had many impressions which saved him the trouble of distinct ideas.
    George Eliot

Imagination

Imagination is more important than knowledge.
    Albert Einstein

The world is but a canvas to our imagination.
    Henry David Thoreau

A man's life is dyed the color of his imagination.
    Marcus Aurelius

The human race is governed by its imagination.
    Napoleon Bonaparte

The world of reality has its limits; the world of imagination is boundless.
    Jean-Jacques Rousseau

Perhaps imagination is only intelligence having fun.
    George Scialabba

To invent, you need a good imagination and a pile of junk.
   Thomas Edison

Only in men's imagination does every truth find an effective and undeniable existence. Imagination, not invention, is the supreme master of art as of life.
   Joseph Conrad

The debt we owe to the play of imagination is incalculable.
   Carl Jung

Imagination has always had powers of resurrection that no science can match.
   Ingrid Bengis

Imagination is the one weapon in the war against reality.
   Jules de Gaultier

To know is nothing at all; to imagine is everything.
   Anatole France

What is now proved was once only imagined.
   William Blake

The imagination is the secret and marrow of civilization. It is the very eye of faith.
   Henry Ward Beecher

If you kill imagination, that is a kind of long-term suicide.
   Pierre Boulez

You can't depend on your judgment when your imagination is out of focus.
   Mark Twain

Imagination is a good horse to carry you over the ground – not a flying carpet to set you free from probability.
   Robertson Davies

Imagination was given to man to compensate him for what he is not; a sense of humor to console him for what he is.
   Francis Bacon

Every nightmare hints at the secret reserves of imaginative power in the human mind.
   John Gardner

Imagination grows by exercise and contrary to common belief is more powerful in the mature than in the young.
   W. Somerset Maugham

Imagination is the true magic carpet.
    Norman Vincent Peale

Our imagination flys…we are its shadow on the earth.
    Vladimir Nabokov

Intellectuals

Like most intellectuals, he is immensely stupid.
    Marquise de Merteuil

An intellectual is a man who doesn't know how to park a bike.
    Spiro Agnew

Intellectuals are the most intolerant of all people.
    Paul Duncun

The difference between western and eastern intellectuals is that the former have not been kicked in the ass enough.
    Witold Gombrowicz

Intellectuals can tell themselves anything, sell themselves any bill of goods, which is why they were so often patsies for the ruling classes.
    Lillian Hellman

Intellectuals are people who believe that ideas are of more importance than values. That is to say, their own ideas and other people's values.
    Gerald Brenan

What is a highbrow? It is a man who has found something more interesting than women.
    Edgar Wallace

Intellectual brilliance is no guarantee against being dead wrong.
    David Fasold

It is not clear that intelligence has any long-term survival value.
    Stephen Hawking

An "egghead" is one who stands firmly on both feet in mid-air on both sides of an issue.
    Homer Ferguson

An intellectual is someone whose mind watches itself.
    Albert Camus

An intellectual is a person who has been educated beyond his intelligence.
Arthur C. Clarke

The course of every intellectual, if he pursues his journey long and unflinchingly enough, ends in the obvious, from which the non-intellectuals have never stirred.
Aldous Huxley

It is always the task of the intellectual to "think otherwise." This is not just a perverse idiosyncrasy. It is an absolutely essential feature of a society.
Harvey Cox

Intellectualism, though by no means confined to doubters, is often the sole piety of the skeptic.
Richard Hofstadter

I hate intellectuals. They are from the top down. I am from the bottom up.
Frank Lloyd Wright

The Journey

A journey of a thousand leagues begins with a single step.
Lao-Tzu

He who is outside the door has already a good part of his journey behind him.
Dutch Proverb

Let no one be deluded that a knowledge of the path can substitute for putting one foot in front of the other.
M.C. Richards

You can't cross the sea merely by staring at the water.
Rabindranath Tagore

The real voyage of discovery consists not in seeking new landscapes but in seeing with new eyes.
Marcel Proust

If a man wishes to be sure of the road he treads on, he must close his eyes and walk in the dark.
Saint John of the Cross

Remember, no matter where you go, there you are.
Peter Weller, The Adventures of Buckaroo Bonzai

It is good to have an end to journey toward; but it is the journey that matters, in the end.
>   Ursula K. Le Guin

All journeys have secret destinations of which the traveler is unaware.
>   Martin Buber

A good Traveler has no fixed plans and is not intent on arriving.
>   Lao-Tzu

To know the road ahead, ask those coming back.
>   Chinese Proverb

The longest journey of any person is the journey inward.
>   Dag Hammerskjöld

All know the way; few actually walk it.
>   Bodhidharma

Two roads diverged into a wood, and I
I took the one less traveled by, and that has made all the difference.
>   Robert Frost

You must choose a road for yourself.
>   Kazuo Koike

If you don't care where you're going, then it doesn't matter which way you go.
>   Lewis Carroll

If you come to a fork in the road, take it.
>   Yogi Berra

I may not have gone where I intended to go, but I think I have ended up where I intended to be.
>   Douglas Adams

The journey is the reward.
>   Taoist Saying

The journey is the greatest part of the destination.
>   Rolling Stone Magazine

The moon and sun are eternal travelers. Even the years wander on...every day is a journey, and the journey itself is home.
>   Basho

You cannot travel on the path until you become the path itself.
>   Buddha

In wonder return to the journey, avail yourself of the path and walk ahead.
Hongzhi Zhengjue

The map is not the territory.
Alfred Korzybski

The first step... shall be to lose the way.
Galway Kinnell

Not all those who wander are lost.
J.R.R. Tolkien

It's easy to get lost in your life.
Raymond Carver

Not until we are lost do we begin to understand ourselves.
Henry David Thoreau

I can't say as ever I was lost, but I was bewildered once for three days.
Daniel Boone

One never goes so far as when one doesn't know where one is going.
Johann Wolfgang von Goethe

Be not afraid of going slowly; be only afraid of standing still.
Chinese Proverb

From a certain point onward there is no longer any turning back. That is the point
that must be reached.
Franz Kafka

Everywhere is walking distance if you have the time.
Stephen Wright

There is nothing like returning to a place that remains unchanged to find the ways in
which you yourself have altered.
Nelson Mandela

Any path is only a path, and there is no affront, to oneself or to others, in dropping it
if that is what your heart tells you.
Carlos Castaneda

There are many paths to the top of the mountain, but the view is always the same.
Chinese Proverb

One does not discover new lands without consenting to lose sight of the shore for
a very long time.
André Gide

Only those who will risk going too far can possibly find out how far one can go.
> T.S. Eliot

A person often meets his destiny on the road he took to avoid it.
> Jean de La Fontaine

There are no shortcuts to any place worth going.
> Beverly Sills

Joy

Scatter Joy.
> Ralph Waldo Emerson

(Man) has given himself over to too little joy. That alone, my brothers, is our original sin. I should believe only in a God who understood how to dance.
> Henri Matisse

Let a joy keep you. Reach out your hands and take it when it runs by.
> Carl Sandburg

He has spent his life best who has enjoyed it most; God will take care that we do not enjoy it any more than is good for us.
> Samuel Butler

Such is human psychology that if we don't express our joy, we soon cease to feel it.
> Lin Yutang

One filled with joy preaches without preaching.
> Mother Teresa

Joy is the serious business of heaven.
> C.S. Lewis

Always remember, joy is not incidental to spiritual quest. It is vital.
> Rebbe Nachman

We all carry it within us; supreme strength, the fullness of wisdom, unquenchable joy.
> Huston Smith

The beating heart of the universe is holy joy.
> Martin Buber

A joyful heart is the inevitable result of a heart burning with love.
> Mother Teresa

I have drunken deep of joy, and I will taste no other wine tonight.
    Percy Bysshe Shelly

The deeper that sorrow carves into your being, the more joy you can contain.
    Kahlil Gibran

We cannot cure the world of sorrows, but we can choose to live in joy.
    Joseph Campbell

One joy scatters a hundred griefs.
    Chinese Proverb

If the day and the night are such that you greet them with joy, and life emits a fragrance like flowers and sweet-scented herbs, that is your success.
    Henry David Thoreau

Joy is but the sign that creative emotion is fulfilling its purpose.
    Charles Du Bos

Joy in looking and comprehending is nature's most beautiful gift.
    Albert Einstein

Joy is not in things; it is in us.
    Richard Wagner

Sometimes your joy is the source of your smile, but sometimes your smile can be the source of your joy.
    Thich Nhat Hanh

A thing of beauty is a joy forever...
    John Keats

The joy that isn't shared dies young.
    Anne Sexton

To look up is joy.
    Confucius

Don't postpone joy.
    Bumper Sticker

Enjoy yourself. It's later than you think.
    Chinese Proverb

Until further notice, celebrate everything.
    Tim Hansel

Kindness

No act of kindness, no matter how small, is ever wasted.
>Aesop

Deeds of kindness are equal in weight to all the commandments.
>The Talmud

The best portion of a good man's life is his little, nameless, unremembered acts of kindness and of love.
>William Wordsworth

Men are only great as they are kind.
>Elbert G. Hubbard

What wisdom can you find that is greater than kindness?
>Jean-Jacques Rousseau

Kindness in words creates confidence. Kindness in thinking creates profoundness. Kindness in giving creates love.
>Lao-Tzu

To cultivate kindness is a valuable part of the business of life.
>Samuel Johnson

Kindness can become its own motive. We are make kind by being kind.
>Eric Hoffer

I expect to pass through life but once. If therefore, there be any kindness I can show... let me do it now.
>William Penn

You can accomplish by kindness what you cannot do by force.
>Publilius Syrus

You can get more with a kind word and a gun than you can with a kind word alone.
>Al Capone

Kind words can be short and easy to speak, but their echoes are truly endless.
>Mother Teresa

Kindness is the mark of faith; and whoever has not kindness has not faith.
>Mohammed

One kind word can warm three winter months.
>Japanese Proverb

Never lose a chance of saying a kind word.
William Makepeace Thackeray

Kindness is the language which the deaf can hear and the blind can see.
Mark Twain

Wherever there is a human being, there is an opportunity for kindness.
Seneca

Men are cruel. Man is kind.
Rabindranath Tagore

Sometimes you must be cruel to be kind.
English Proverb

If you can't be kind, at least be vague.
Judith Martin, a.k.a. Miss Manners

One can pay back the loan of gold, but one lies forever in debt to those who are kind.
Malayan Proverb

Forget injuries, never forget kindness.
Confucius

Kindness consists in loving people more than they deserve.
Jacqueline Schiff

Constant kindness can accomplish much. As the sun makes ice melt, kindness causes misunderstanding, mistrust, and hostility to evaporate.
Albert Schweitzer

Kindness is more important than wisdom, and the recognition of this is the beginning of wisdom.
Theodore Isaac Rubin

The highest wisdom is loving kindness.
The Talmud

Knowledge

No knowledge comes from outside; it is all inside.
Swami Vivekananda

When you understand one thing through and through, you understand everything.
Shunryu Suzuki Roshi

The knowledge beyond knowledge is my knowledge.
Kabir

It is only when we forget all our learning that we begin to know.
Henry David Thoreau

Everything you know is wrong.
Firesign Theatre

The first step to knowledge is to know that we are ignorant.
Lord David Cecil

I don't wanna be a pinhead no more.
Joey Ramone

The greater our knowledge increases, the greater our ignorance unfolds.
John F. Kennedy

The more I learn, the more I realize I don't know.
Albert Einstein

What do I know?
Michel de Montaigne

I do not know what I do not know.
Ludwig Wittgenstein

The first and wisest of them all professed
To know this only, that he nothing knew.
John Milton

Lack of true knowledge is the source of all pains and sorrows.
Yoga Sutras

I am still learning.
Michelangelo's Motto

I am not young enough to know everything.
Sir James M. Barrie

To know all things is not permitted.
 Horace

After such knowledge, what forgiveness?
 T.S. Eliot

Everyone is ignorant, only on different subjects.
 Will Rogers

His ignorance is encyclopedic.
 Abba Eban

There is much pleasure to be gained from useless knowledge.
 Bertrand Russell

Rather know nothing than half-know much.
 Friedrich Nietzsche

Knowledge is knowing as little as possible
 Charles Bukowski

If a little knowledge is dangerous, when is the man who has so much as to be out of danger?
 Thomas Henry Huxley

The greatest obstacle to discovery is not ignorance – it is the illusion of knowledge.
 Daniel J. Boorstin

To be proud of knowledge is to be blind with light.
 Benjamin Franklin

Knowing is half the battle.
 G.I. Joe

We are here and it is now. Further than that, all human knowledge is moonshine.
 H.L. Mencken

He that increaseth knowledge increaseth sorrow.
 Bible, Ecclesiastes 1:18

It is not a question how much a man knows, but what use he can make of what he knows.
 J.G. Holland

He who does not know one thing, knows another.
 Kenyan Proverb

You can know ten things by learning one.
Japanese proverb

I'm astounded by people who want to "know" the universe when it's hard enough to find your way around Chinatown.
Woody Allen

I do not pretend to understand the universe. It's a great deal bigger than I am.
Tom Stoppard

Do not learn more than you absolutely need to get through life.
Karl Kraus

A fool will learn nothing from a wise man, but a wise man will learn much from a fool.
Lao-Tzu

An investment in knowledge always pays the best interest.
Benjamin Franklin

The roots of knowledge are bitter, but its fruit are sweet.
Marcus Tullius Cicero

Knowledge is power.
Francis Bacon

Accumulate learning by study, understand what you learn by questioning.
Cha'n Master Mingjiao

Education is an admirable thing, but it is well to remember from time to time that nothing that is worth knowing can be taught.
Oscar Wilde

We are torn between the craving to know and the despair of having known.
Carl Sagan

Knowledge is the true organ of sight, not the eyes.
Panchatantra

The desire of knowledge, like the thirst of riches, increases ever with the acquisition of it.
Laurence Sterne

All that we know is nothing, we are merely crammed wastepaper baskets, unless we are in touch with that which laughs at all our knowing.
D.H. Lawrence

Life

It's life, Jim... but not as we know it.
  Spock

Life is neither a spectacle nor a feast; it is a predicament.
  George Santayana

Life is the art of drawing sufficient conclusions from insufficient premises.
  Samuel Butler

Life is just one damned thing after another.
  Elbert G. Hubbard

Life is a dream; the awakening kills us.
  Virginia Woolf

Life is hard. After all, it kills you.
  Katherine Hepburn

We cannot truly face life until we face the fact that it will be taken away from us.
  Billy Graham

All the arts we practice are an apprenticeship. The big art is our life.
  M.C. Richards

There is more to life than increasing its speed.
  Mahatma Gandhi

That it will never come again is what makes life so sweet.
  Emily Dickinson

What you get is a living; what you give is a life.
  Lillian Gish

The great use of life is to spend it for something that will outlast it.
  William James

Life itself is the proper binge.
  Julia Child

Life is a gamble at terrible odds, if it were a bet, you would not take it.
  Tom Stoppard

I take a simple view of life: keep your eyes open and get on with it.
  Sir Laurence Olivier

In three words I can sum up everything I've learned about life. It goes on.
Robert Frost

Life is a horizontal fall.
Jean Cocteau

People find life entirely too time-consuming.
Stanislaw J. Lec

Life is like a box of sardines and we are all looking for the key.
Alan Bennett

Life is full of misery, loneliness, and suffering – and it's all over much too soon.
Woody Allen

Life is a tale told by an idiot – full of sound and fury, signifying nothing.
William Shakespeare

Our life, to what shall I compare it? An echo echoing through the mountains and into empty sky.
Ryokän

Life is short; live it up.
Nikita Khrushchev

Life is a dead-end street.
H.L. Mencken

Life is a toy made of glass; it appears to be of inestimable price, but in reality it is very cheap.
Pietro Aretino

Men must live and create. Live to the point of tears.
Albert Camus

Life consists in what a man is thinking of all day.
Ralph Waldo Emerson

Our life is what our thoughts make it.
Marcus Aurelius

Life is like an onion, which one peels crying.
French Proverb

Life is not having been told that the man has just waxed the floor.
Ogden Nash

Life is too short for men to take it seriously.
George Bernard Shaw

Life is a tragedy when seen in close-up, but a comedy in long-shot
Charlie Chaplin

Life is a moderately good play with a badly written third act.
Truman Capote

My life has a superb cast but I can't figure out the plot.
Ashleigh Brilliant

Life is like Sanskrit read to a pony.
Lou Reed

Life is a disease, sexually transmitted and always fatal.
Noah George

Life is an incurable disease.
Abraham Cowley

Life is thirst.
Leonard Michaels

Life's neither good nor evil: it's a field for good and evil.
Seneca

Life is perhaps most wisely regarded as a bad dream between two awakenings, and everyday is a life in miniature.
Eugene O'Neill

We cannot put off living until we are ready...Life is fired at us point-blank.
José Ortega y Gasset

Life is not a dress rehearsal.
Rose Tremain

Life may have no meaning. Or even worse, it may have a meaning of which I disapprove.
Ashleigh Brilliant

There is no meaning to life except the meaning man gives to his life by the unfolding of his powers.
Erich Fromm

The meaning of life is to see.
Hui-Neng

There are two great disappointments in life. Not getting what you want and getting it.
 George Bernard Shaw

The first duty of life is to assume a pose. What the second is, no one has yet discovered.
 Oscar Wilde

Life is picking up a girl with bad teeth, or getting to know one of those wild-eyed rummies down on Sixth Avenue.
 Tom Waits

True life is lived when tiny changes occur.
 Leo Tolstoy

Life is like music; it must be composed by ear, feeling, and instinct, not by rule.
 Samuel Butler

What we play is life.
 Louis Armstrong

Live your own life, for you will die your own death.
 Latin Proverb

Life is just a party, and parties weren't meant 2 last.
 Prince

Life was a funny thing that happened to me on the way to the grave.
 Quentin Crisp

Life is what happens to you while you are busy making other plans.
 John Lennon

Life is something to do when you can't get to sleep.
 Fran Lebowitz

Life is but a dream.
 Row, Row, Row Your Boat

Life is a dream, but don't wake me.
 Yiddish proverb

Life is like a voyage that is homeward bound.
 Herman Melville

Life is like playing a violin in public and learning the instrument as one goes on.
 Samuel Butler

Life is the only game in which the object of the game is to learn the rules.
Ashleigh Brilliant

Life must be lived and curiosity kept alive. One must never, for whatever reason, turn his back on life.
Eleanor Roosevelt

Life is a perpetual instruction in cause and effect.
Ralph Waldo Emerson

Life can only be understood backwards, but it must be lived forwards.
Søren Kierkegaard

Life is a series of relapses and recoveries.
George Ade

Life has changed into a timeless succession of shocks, interspaced with empty, paralyzed intervals.
Theodor W. Adorno

Life is a long lesson in humility.
Sir James M. Barrie

Life is as tedious as a twice-told tale.
William Shakespeare

Life is one long process of getting tired.
Samuel Butler

When I hear somebody sigh, Life is hard, I am always tempted to ask, Compared to what?
Sydney J. Harris

Life is not meant to be easy, my child; but take courage – it can be delightful.
George Bernard Shaw

From what we get, we make a living; what we live, however, makes a life.
Arthur Ashe

Life isn't about finding yourself, it's about creating yourself.
George Bernard Shaw

Life is not giving up, but moving on.
Martha Graham

Life, according to Zen, ought to be lived as a bird flies through the air, or as a fish swims in the water.
D.T. Suzuki

Life is either a daring adventure, or nothing.
>   Helen Keller

One's only real life is the life one never leads.
>   Oscar Wilde

Life is like nothing I've ever seen.
>   Arthur Penn

Life is the sum of all your choices.
>   Albert Camus

Life is better than death, I believe, if only because it is less boring, and because it has fresh peaches in it.
>   Alice Walker

Life is a game at which everybody loses.
>   Leo Sarkadi-Schuller

Life is a funny thing that occurs on the way to the grave.
>   Quentin Crisp

Life is something that everyone should try at least once.
>   Henry J. Tillman

All animals except man know that the principal business of life is to enjoy it.
>   Samuel Butler

Life is a zoo in a jungle.
>   Peter DeVries

Life's under no obligation to give us what we expect.
>   Margaret Mitchell

Life does not have to be perfect to be wonderful.
>   Annette Funicello

My life is my message.
>   Mahatma Gandhi

We must be willing to get rid of the life we've planned, so as to have the life that is waiting for us.
>   Joseph Campbell

And life is what we make it. Always has been, always will be.
>   Grandma Moses

Living

Walking the wire is living. The rest is just waiting.
>Karl Wallenda, a few weeks before he fell to his death in 1978

People living deeply have no fear of death.
>Anaïs Nin

To live fully is to let go and die with each passing moment, and to be reborn in each new one.
>Jack Kornfield

To live is to be slowly born.
>Antoine de Saint-Exupéry

I must live until I die.
>Joseph Conrad

There is no cure for birth and death save to enjoy the interval.
>George Santayana

When we were born we cried and the people around us smiled. Live life so that when you die you are smiling and the people around you are crying.
>Nelson Mandela

There are only two ways to live your life. One is as though nothing is a miracle. The other is as though everything is a miracle.
>Albert Einstein

You only live once – but if you work it right, once is enough.
>Joe E. Lewis

Live as though it were your last day on earth. Some day you will be right.
>Robert Anthony

Most of us spend our lives as if we had another one in the bank.
>Ben Irwin

I came into this world, not chiefly to make this a good place to live in, but to live in it, be it good or bad.
>Henry David Thoreau

Living Well Is The Best Revenge.
>Calvin Thomas

Remember to live.
>Johann Wolfgang von Goethe

A person starts to live when he can live outside himself.
  Albert Einstein

The art of living lies not in eliminating but in growing with troubles.
  Bernard M. Baruch

The art of living is more like wrestling than dancing.
  Marcus Aurelius

Learning to live is learning to let go.
  Sogyal Rinpoche

As long as you live, keep learning how to live.
  Seneca

One lives in the hope of becoming a memory.
  Antonio Porchia

Living is like walking on thin ice.
  Confucius

Everything has been figured out, except how to live.
  Jean-Paul Sartre

Just breathing isn't living.
  Pollyanna

The proper function of man is to live, not to exist.
  Jack London

We think in generalities, we live in detail.
  Alfred North Whitehead

To live is so startling it leaves little time for anything else.
  Emily Dickinson

If you ask me what I have come to do in this world … I will reply: I'm here to live
my life out loud.
  Émile Zola

We are in this life to enlarge the soul, liberate the spirit, and light up the brain.
  Tom Robbins

He who has a why to live can bear with almost any how.
  Fredrich Nietzsche

Any idiot can face a crisis, it is the day-to-day living that wears you out.
  Anton Chekhov

If you suffer, thank God! It is a sure sign that you are alive.
> Elbert G. Hubbard

I have sometimes been wildly, despairingly, acutely miserable, racked with sorrow, but through it all I still know quite certainly that just to be alive is a grand thing.
> Agatha Christie

Be not afraid of life. Believe that life is worth living, and your belief will help create that fact.
> William James

I don't believe people are looking for the meaning of life as much as they are looking for the experience of being alive.
> Joseph Campbell

I don't want to get to the end of my life and find that I have just lived the length of it. I want to have lived the width of it as well.
> Diane Ackerman

Love

We cannot do great things on this earth. We can only do little things with great love.
> Mother Teresa

Where there is great love there are always miracles.
> Willa Cather

Immerse your soul in love.
> Thom Yorke

With our love, we could save the world.
> George Harrison

To love someone is to see a miracle invisible to others.
> Francois Mauriac

With love and patience, nothing is impossible.
> Daisaku Ikeda

Love is the pursuit of the whole.
> Plato

The Eskimos had fifty-two names for snow because it was important to them; there ought to be as many for love.
> Margaret Atwood

Love cures people. Both the ones who give it, and the ones who receive it.
    Karl Menniger

Love is above all, the gift of oneself.
    Jean Anouilh

Love is a power too strong to be overcome by anything but flight.
    Miguel de Cervantes

There is hardly any activity, any enterprise, which is started with such tremendous hopes and expectations, and yet which fails so regularly, as love.
    Erich Fromm

Love is like a card trick – once you learn how it's done, you can't be fooled any longer.
    Fanny Brice

Love is only the dirty trick played on us to achieve continuation of the species.
    W. Somerset Maugham

Love is the triumph of imagination over intelligence.
    H.L. Mencken

Love is a dangerous necessity.
    Charles Mingus

When love is not madness, it is not love.
    Pedro Calderón de la Barca

Love is insanity with a collaborator.
    Gene Perret

It is impossible to love and be wise.
    Francis Bacon

The greatest love is a mother's; then comes a dog's; then comes a sweetheart's.
    Polish Proverb

All you need is love
    John Lennon

The greatest thing you'll ever learn is just to love and be loved in return
    Eden Ahbez

Love does not just sit there, like a stone; it has to be made, like bread, remade all the time, made new.
    Ursula K. Le Guin

We are shaped and fashioned by what we love.
Johann Wolfgang von Goethe

What you love is a sign from your higher self of what you are to do.
Sanaya Roman

True love is like ghosts, which everybody talks about and few have seen.
François duc de la Rochefoucauld

They love too much that die for love.
English Proverb

The great tragedy of life is not that men perish, but that they cease to love.
W. Somerset Maugham

I don't want to live – I want to love first, and live incidentally.
Zelda Fitzgerald

There is no remedy for love but to love more.
Henry David Thoreau

The one thing we can never get enough of is love. And the one thing we never give
enough is love.
Henry Miller

Love is like longing, and energy. It's like magnetism, it's like gravity. And at its
highest it's about spiritual salvation.
Pete Townshend

One must learn to love and go through a good deal of suffering to get to it, and the
journey is always towards the soul.
D.H. Lawrence

Love, having no geography, knows no boundaries.
Truman Capote

Love ... is the extremely difficult realization that something other than oneself is real.
Iris Murdoch

Anyone can hate. It costs to love.
John Williamson

Love is a hole in the heart.
Ben Hecht

Where there is love, there is pain.
Spanish Proverb

One word frees us off all the weight and pain of life. That word is love.
    Sophocles

You will find as you look back upon your life that the moments when you have truly lived are the moments when you have done things in the spirit of love.
    Henry Drummond

Love is the distance between reality and pain.
    Robin Hitchcock

Loves conquers all things except poverty and toothache.
    Mae West

Love is colder than death.
    Rainer Werner Fassbinder

It is love, not reason, that is stronger than death.
    Thomas Mann

To fall in love is to create a religion that has a fallible god.
    Jorge Luis Borges

God is love – I dare say. But what a mischievous devil love is.
    Samuel Butler

To love another person is to see the face of God.
    Victor Hugo

What is important is that one is capable of love. It is perhaps the only glimpse we are permitted of eternity.
    Helen Hayes

Love makes the time pass. Time makes the love pass.
    French Proverb

Great love can both take hold and let go.
    O.R. Orage

The way to love anything is to realize that it might be lost.
    G.K. Chesterton

Love is the greatest of all human gifts for it allows us to look upon one another the way God surely must see us all.
    Jorge Luis Borges

Love is a mystery which when solved, evaporates. The same holds for music.
    Ned Rorem

Love is like quick-silver in the hand. Leave the fingers open and it stays. Clutch it, and it darts away.
      Dorothy Parker

Love is much like a wild rose, beautiful and calm, but willing to draw blood in its defense.
      Mark Overby

Love is like war; easy to begin but very hard to stop.
      H.L. Mencken

Love like a tear, rises in the eye and falls upon the breast.
      Publilius Syrus

The only abnormality is the incapacity to love.
      Anaïs Nin

We love because it's the only true adventure.
      Nikki Giovanni

Love is the wisdom of the fool and the folly of the wise.
      H.L. Mencken

The first duty of love is to listen.
      Paul Johannes Tillich

If love is the answer, could you rephrase the question?
      Lily Tomlin

Love is a fire. But whether it is going to warm your hearth or burn down your house, you can never tell.
      Joan Crawford

Love in its essence is spiritual fire.
      Emanuel Swedenborg

Love is a smoke made with the fume of sighs.
      William Shakespeare

Love is an exploding cigar we willingly smoke.
      Lynda Barry

Magic

Disbelief in magic can force a poor soul into believing in government and business.
  Tom Robbins

The magic theater is not for everyone.
   Hermann Hesse

Magic embodies the concept of lying turned into an art form.
   Teller of Penn & Teller

Genius is another word for magic, and the whole point of magic is that it
is inexplicable.
   Margot Fonteyn

The universe is full of magical things, patiently waiting for our wits to grow sharper.
   Eden Phillpotts

The greatest secrets are always hidden in the most unlikely places. Those who don't
believe in magic will never find it.
   Roald Dahl

Magic is something we do to ourselves.
   Aleister Crowley

There's a bit of magic in everything, and some loss to even things out.
   Lou Reed

Snatching the eternal out of the desperately fleeting is the great magic trick of
human existence.
   Tennessee Williams

One man's "magic" is another man's engineering, "Supernatural" is a null word.
   Robert Heinlein

We ourselves cannot put any magic spell on this world. The world is its own magic.
   Shunryu Suzuki Roshi

Using words to describe magic is like using a screwdriver to cut roast beef.
   Tom Robbins

Men

Men have a much better time of it than women; for one thing, they marry later; for another thing they die earlier.
H.L. Mencken

Not only is it harder to be a man, it is also harder to become one.
Arianna Stassinopoulos

Are we not men?
Mark Mothersbaugh

Men cease to interest us when we find their limitations.
Ralph Waldo Emerson

Men are happy to be laughed at for their humor, but not for their folly.
Jonathan Swift

There must be some reason why a man must be convinced, while a woman must be persuaded.
Robert B. Fleming

Women like silent men. They think they're listening.
Marcel Archard

The most important thing in a relationship between a man and a woman is that one of them must be good at taking orders.
Linda Festa

A man in the house is worth two in the street.
Mae West

Man is not the enemy here, but the fellow victim.
Betty Friedan

There are more things in men to admire than despise.
Albert Camus

It is a man's world, and you men can have it.
Katherine Anne Porter

I require three things in a man: He must be handsome, ruthless, and stupid.
Dorothy Parker

Men are irrelevant.
Fay Weldon

Most men do not mature, they simply grow taller.
Leo Rosten

Men are nicotine soaked, beer besmirched, whiskey greased, red-eyed devils.
Carry Nation

All men are intrinsical rascals, and I am only sorry that not being a dog
I can't bite them.
Lord Byron

Men are no more than mischievous baboons.
Dr. William Harvey

It's not the men in my life, it's the life in my men.
Mae West

Money

Money is like sex. It seems much more important if you don't have any.
Charles Bukowski

Some men worship rank, some worship heroes, some worship power, some worship
God, and over these ideals they dispute – but they all worship money.
Mark Twain

Too many people spend money they haven't earned, to buy things they don't want,
to impress people they don't like.
Will Rogers

Never spend your money before you have it.
Thomas Jefferson

Money is a good servant but a bad master.
Francis Bacon

Money often costs too much.
Ralph Waldo Emerson

I have always treated money as the stuff with which one purchases time.
Tom Stoppard

If you want to know what God thinks of money, just look at the people he gave it to.
Dorothy Parker

As a general rule, nobody has money who ought to have it.
Benjamin Franklin

Money can't buy friends, but you can get a better class of enemy.
Spike Milligan

The only thing I like about rich people is their money.
Lady Astor

Follow the money.
W. Mark Felt (aka Deep Throat), on the Watergate investigation

Fortune does not change men, it unmasks them.
Suzanne Necker

Gold is tested by fire, man by gold.
Chinese Proverb

Money is better than poverty, if only for financial reasons.
Woody Allen

The real measure of your wealth is how much you'd be worth if you lost all your money.
Unknown

The value of money is that with it you can tell anyone to go to the devil.
W. Somerset Maugham

I feel the closest to Hell when I'm thinking about money.
Pharaoh Sanders

I finally know what distinguishes man from the other beasts: financial worries.
Jules Renard

I have no money, no resources, no hopes. I am the happiest man alive.
Henry Miller

A rich person is one who has enough.
Chinese Proverb

The rich worry over their money, the poor over their bread.
Vietnamese Proverb

There is no man so poor as he who has only money.
Edwin Pugh

He who knows how to be poor knows everything.
Jules Michelet

The love of money is the root of all evil.
Bible, 1 Timothy 6:10

The lack of money is the root of all evil.
George Bernard Shaw

No one can earn a million dollars honestly.
William Jennings Bryan

Behind every great fortune there is a crime.
Honore de Balzac

If you can count your money, you don't have a billion dollars.
J. Paul Getty

What this country needs is a good five-cent nickel.
Frank Adams

Money, young man, is good for the nerves.
J.P. Morgan

If someone says "It's not the money, it's the principle," it's the money.
Angelo Valenti

Every man has his price, what's yours?
Jimmy Hoffa

I don't like money, actually, but it quiets my nerves.
Joe Louis

I'm living so far beyond my income that we may almost be said to be living apart.
e.e. cummings

All I ask is a chance to prove that money can't make me happy.
Ashleigh Brilliant

It is odd, is it not, that a person's worth to society is measured by their wealth,
when instead their wealth should be measured by their worth to society.
A. Cygni

The chief value of money lies in the fact that one lives in a world in which
it is overestimated.
Henry Lewis Mencken

They who are of the opinion that money will do everything, may very well be
suspected to do everything for money.
George Savile, Marquis of Halifax

Money doesn't mind if we say it's evil, it goes from strength to strength.
It's a fiction, an addiction, and a tacit conspiracy.
Martin Amis

The amount of money one needs is terrifying.
Ludwig Von Beethoven

The most efficient labor-saving device is still money.
Franklin P. Jones

If a rich man is proud of his wealth, he should not be praised until it is known how he employs it.
Socrates

It is easier for a camel to go through the eye of a needle, than for a rich man to enter into the kingdom of God.
Matthew 19:24

The man who dies rich dies disgraced.
Andrew Carnegie

It is in spending oneself that one becomes rich.
Sarah Bernhardt

I've got all the money I'll ever need, just as long as I die by four o'clock.
Henny Youngman

A man with money is no match against a man on a mission.
Doyle Brunson

Money is what people without talent use to keep score.
Jeremy C. Epworth

If all you want to do is make money, the very last thing you need is imagination.
James Baldwin

Money, like dung, does no good till 'tis spread.
Dr. Thomas Fuller

Money is ideologically pure. It sullies everyone equally and therefore can't be sullied by anyone.
Simon Kunan

Money talks because money is a metaphor, a transfer, and a bridge.
Marshall McLuhan

When money speaks, the truth keeps silent.
Russian Proverb

Money doesn't talk, it swears.
Bob Dylan

With money in your pocket, you are wise and you are handsome and you
sing well too.
> Yiddish Proverb

Because that's where the money is.
> Ascribed to Willie Sutton, when asked why he robbed banks

Music

After silence, that which comes closest to expressing the inexpressible is music.
> Aldous Huxley

A painter paints pictures on canvas. But musicians paint their pictures on silence.
> Leopold Stokowski

Music is the wine that fills the cup of silence.
> Robert Fripp

Music must take rank as the highest of the fine arts – as the one which, more than
any other, ministers to the human spirit.
> Herbert Spencer

Where there's music there can be no evil.
> Miguel de Cervantes

Music is well said to be the speech of angels.
> Thomas Carlyle

God tells me how the music should sound, but you stand in the way.
> Arturo Toscanini to a trumpet player

Music is a higher revelation than philosophy.
> Ludwig van Beethoven

Music has the charms to soothe a savage beast – but not the unmusical one.
> Alexander Chase

Not everything in music is audible.
> Charles Rosen

Wagner's music is better than it sounds.
> Mark Twain

Of all noises, I think music is the least disagreeable.
> Samuel Johnson

Too many pieces of music finish too long after the end.
Igor Stravinsky

Often I am still listening when the song is over.
Marquis de Saint-Lambert

The high note is not the only thing.
Placido Domingo

You can play a shoestring if you're sincere.
John Coltrane

Good music is very close to primitive language.
Denis Diderot

Where words fail, music speaks.
Hans Christian Andersen

If music could be translated into human speech, it would no longer need to exist.
Ned Rorem

Music is a controlled outcry from the quarry of emotions all humans share.
Diane Ackerman

There is nothing more difficult than talking about music.
Camille Saint-Saëns

Talking about music is like dancing about architecture.
Steve Martin

Architecture is frozen music.
Johann Wolfgang von Goethe

My music is best understood by children and animals.
Igor Stravinsky

I don't know anything about music. In my line you don't have to.
Elvis Presley

The music business is a cruel and shallow money trench where thieves and pimps run free and good men die like dogs. There's also a negative side.
Hunter S. Thompson

Music has charms to soothe a savage breast, to soften rocks, or bend a knotted oak.
William Congreve

Music rearranges your molecular structure.
Carlos Santana

138

Music melts all the separate parts of our bodies together.
Anaïs Nin

Music is the only sensual pleasure without vice.
Samuel Johnson

Children of the night, what music they make.
Count Dracula

The difference between a violin and a viola is that a viola burns longer.
Victor Borge

Music is the art which is most nigh to tears and memory.
Oscar Wilde

Most people wouldn't know good music if it came up and bit them in the ass.
Frank Zappa

Extraordinary how potent cheap music is.
Noel Coward

Only sick music makes money today.
Friedrich Nietzsche

All music jars when the soul's out of tune.
Miguel de Cervantes

Music is a beautiful opiate, if you don't take it too seriously.
Henry Miller

Music is the sole domain in which man realizes the present.
Igor Stravinsky

Music should never be harmless.
Robbie Robertson

If a young man at the age of twenty-three can write a symphony like that, in five years he will be ready to commit murder.
Walter Damrosch, describing Aaron Copland

One good thing about music... when it hits you feel no pain... so hit me with music.
Bob Marley

Music heard so deeply that it is not heard at all, but you are the music while the music lasts.
T.S. Eliot

If you cannot teach me to fly, teach me to sing.
Sir James M. Barrie

Without music, life would be a mistake
Friedrich Nietzsche

Mystery

The most beautiful thing we can experience is the mysterious. It is the source of all true art and science.
Albert Einstein

Until we accept the fact that life itself is founded in mystery, we shall learn nothing.
Henry Miller

Wisdom and deep intelligence require an honest appreciation of mystery.
Thomas Moore

Those who dwell among the beauties and mysteries of the earth are never alone or weary of life.
Rachel Carson

Mystery has its own mysteries, and there are gods above gods. We have ours, they have theirs. That is what's known as infinity.
Jean Cocteau

The possession of knowledge does not kill the sense of wonder and mystery. There is always more mystery.
Anaïs Nin

It's a mystery wrapped in a riddle inside an enigma.
David Ferrie, on the JFK assissination

Every mystery solved brings us to the threshold of a greater one.
Rachel Carson

As we acquire more knowledge, things do not become more comprehensible, but more mysterious.
Albert Schweitzer

Mystifications protect power, mysteries protect the sacred.
John Berger

The true mystery of the world is the visible, not the invisible.
Oscar Wilde

A perception, sudden as blinking, that subject and object are one, will lead
to a deeply mysterious understanding; and by this understanding you will awaken
to the truth.
>Huang Po

Mysteries are not necessarily miracles.
>Johann Wolfgang von Goethe

Each time dawn appears, the mystery is there in its entirety.
>Reni Daumal

The mystery of life is not a problem to solve but a reality to experience.
>Frank Herbert

When a mystery is too overpowering, one dare not disobey.
>Antoine de Saint-Exupéry

It began in mystery, and it will end in mystery, but what a savage and beautiful
country lies in between.
>Diane Ackerman

Now comes the mystery.
>Henry Ward Beecher's last words, March 8, 1887

Mystery creates wonder and wonder is the basis of man's desire to understand.
>Neil Armstrong

Mystery is underrated, and understanding is overrated.
>Larry McMurtry

The ultimate gift of conscious life is a sense of the mystery that encompasses it.
>Lewis Mumford

There's a natural mystic floating through the air.
>Bob Marley

I would rather live in a world where my life is surrounded by mystery than live in a
world so small that my mind could comprehend it.
>Henry Emerson Fosdick

Let the mind be enlarged to the grandeur of the mysteries, and not the mysteries
contracted to the narrowness of the mind.
>Francis Bacon

The trick is not to live in the know but to live in the mystery.
>Dr. Fred Alan Wolf

It was the experience of mystery – even if mixed with fear – that engendered religion.
    Albert Einstein

The final mystery is oneself.
    Oscar Wilde

Order

What we imagine is order is merely the prevailing form of chaos.
    Kerry Thornley

Crude classifications and false generalizations are the curse of the organized life.
    H.G. Wells

One of the advantages of being disorderly is that one is constantly making exciting discoveries.
    A.A. Milne

One can't live in a house too well kept. One has to go off into the jungle to find simpler ways which won't stifle the spirit.
    Henri Matisse

I tell you: one must still have chaos in one, to give birth to a dancing star.
    Friedrich Nietzsche

Chaos demands to be recognized and experienced before letting itself be converted into a new order.
    Hermann Hesse

There are always many more disordered than ordered systems.
    Second Law of Thermodynamics

Good order is the foundation of all things.
    Edmund Burke

Perfect order is the forerunner of perfect horror.
    Carlos Fuentes

The world is not to be put in order; the world is order, incarnate. It is for us to harmonize with this order.
    Henry Miller

Chaos often breeds life, when order breeds habit.
    Henry Brooks Adams

142

Chaos is a friend of mine.
>Bob Dylan

Watch out for the fellow who talks about putting things in order! Putting things in order always means getting other people under your control.
>Denis Diderot

The whole order of things is as outrageous as any miracle which could presume to violate it.
>G.K. Chesterton

Chaos in the midst of chaos isn't funny, but chaos in the midst of order is.
>Steve Martin

Order is the shape upon which beauty depends.
>Pearl S. Buck

A place for everything, everything in its place.
>Benjamin Franklin

No snowflake falls in an inappropriate place.
>Zen Saying

Order and simplification are the first steps toward the mastery of a subject.
>Thomas Mann

In my youth I stressed freedom, and in my old age I stress order. I have made the great discovery that liberty is a product of order.
>Will Durant

Order marches with weighty and measured strides; disorder is always in a hurry.
>Napoleon Bonaparte

Some people like to make a little garden out of life and walk down a path.
>Jean Anouilh

The formula "Two and two make five" is not without its attractions.
>Fyodor Dostoevsky

Well if a six turned out to be nine. I don't mind. I don't mind.
>Jimi Hendrix

Let all things be done decently and in order.
>Bible, 1 Corinthians 14:40

Passion

All passions exaggerate: it is only because they exaggerate that they are passions.
Sébastien Chamfort

Nothing that is not the product of obsession can be worthwhile.
Michelangelo

All humanity is passion; without passion, religion, history, novels, art would be ineffectual.
Honore de Balzac

Passion, I see, is catching.
William Shakespeare

There is no end. There is no beginning. There is only the infinite passion of life.
Fedrico Fellini

His passions make man live, his wisdom merely makes him last.
Sébastien Chamfort

I know that I have found fulfillment. I have an object in life, a task, a – let me be frank and say a passion.
George Sand

Passion costs me too much to bestow it on every trifle.
Thomas Adams

My passions were all gathered together like fingers that made a fist. Drive is considered aggression today; I knew it then as purpose.
Bette Davis

Passions elevate the soul to great things.
Denis Diderot

A man in a passion rides a horse that runs away with him.
Dr. Thomas Fuller

If passion drives you, let reason hold the reins.
Benjamin Franklin

Passions are the gales of life.
Alexander Pope

The most powerful weapon on earth is the human soul on fire.
Ferdinand Foch

Passions are vices or virtues to their highest powers.
Johann Wolfgang von Goethe

Anyone who seeks to destroy the passions instead of controlling them is trying to play the angel.
Voltaire

It is difficult to lay aside a confirmed passion.
Caius Valerius Catullus

Without passion man is a mere latent force and possibility, like the flint which awaits the shock of the iron before it can give forth its spark.
Henri-Frederic Amiel

If you follow your bliss, doors will open for you that wouldn't have opened for anyone else.
Joseph Campbell

Our passions are ourselves.
Anatole France

Peace

Peace comes from within. Do not seek it without.
Buddha

Nothing can bring you peace but yourself.
Ralph Waldo Emerson

Without inner peace, it is impossible to have world peace.
Tenzin Gyatso, 14th Dalai Lama

None is richer than he who simply has peace of mind.
Maj Wambebe

Peace is the first condition without which nothing can be stable.
Sri Aurobindo

Peace is not merely the absence of war. It is also a state of mind. Lasting peace can come only to peaceful people.
Jawaharlal Nehru

Only in quiet waters do thing mirror themselves undistorted. Only in a quiet mind is adequate perception of the world.
Hans Margolius

We shall find peace. We shall hear angels. We shall see the sky sparkling with diamonds.
> Anton Chekhov

We are going to have peace even if we have to fight for it.
> Dwight D. Eisenhower

If we have no peace, it is because we have forgotten that we belong to each other.
> Mother Teresa

There is no way to peace, peace is the way.
> A.J. Muste

If there is to be any peace it will come through being, not having.
> Henry Miller

Peace is when time doesn't matter as it passes by.
> Maria Schell

It is easier to lead men to combat, stirring up their passion, than to restrain them and direct them toward the patient labors of peace.
> André Gide

An unjust peace is better than a just war.
> Marcus Tullius Cicero

Peace cannot be achieved through violence, it can only be attained through understanding.
> Ralph Waldo Emerson

All we are saying is give peace a chance.
> John Lennon

Peace is not merely a distant goal that we seek, but a means by which we arrive at that goal.
> Martin Luther King, Jr.

What's so funny about peace, love and understanding?
> Elvis Costello

Perseverance

That which doesn't kill me, makes me stronger.
>Fredrich Neitzsche

A series of failures may culminate in the best possible result.
>Gisela Richter

The best way out is always through.
>Robert Frost

God is with those who persevere.
>The Koran

Perseverance, n. A lowly virtue whereby mediocrity achieves an inglorious success.
>Ambrose Bierce, The Devil's Dictionary

Great works are performed not by strength but by perseverance.
>Samuel Johnson

He conquers who endures.
>Persius

Many strokes overthrow the tallest oaks.
>John Lyly

Perseverance is not a long race; it is many short races one after another.
>Walter Elliott

To endure is the first thing that a child ought to learn, and that which he will have the most need to know.
>Jean-Jacques Rousseau

Most people never run far enough on their first wind to find out they've got a second.
>William James

When you have exhausted all possibilities, remember this – You haven't.
>Thomas Edison

A set back is the opportunity to begin again more intelligently.
>Henry Ford

Fall seven times and stand up eight.
>Japanese Proverb

You just can't beat the person who never gives up.
>Babe Ruth

I have not failed. I've just found 10,000 ways that won't work.
  Thomas Edison

Effort only fully releases its reward after a person refuses to quit.
  Napoleon Hill

Pray to God, but hammer away.
  Spanish Proverb

Power

Power is the ultimate aphrodisiac.
  Henry Kissinger

All I want is a warm bed and a kind word and unlimited power.
  Ashleigh Brilliant

The lust for power is not rooted in strength but in weakness.
  Erich Fromm

Power corrupts, and absolute power corrupts absolutely.
  Lord Acton

Power corrupts. Absolute power is kind of neat.
  John Lehman, Secretary of the Navy, 1981-1987

Power doesn't corrupt people, people corrupt power.
  William Gaddis

Nearly all men can stand adversity, but if you want to test a man's character,
give him power.
  Abraham Lincoln

No man is wise enough nor good enough to be trusted with unlimited power.
  Charles Caleb Colton

My opinion is, that power should always be distrusted, in whatever hands
it is placed.
  Sir William Jones

Power is not revealed by striking hard and striking often, but by striking true.
  Honore de Balzac

In any contest between power and patience, bet on patience.
  W.B. Prescott

Power can be taken, but not given. The process of the taking is empowerment in itself.
Gloria Steinem

I know of nothing sublime which is not some modification of power.
Edmund Burke

The most common way people give up their power is by thinking they don't have any.
Alice Walker

The side without power is always the side that is accused of being irrational.
Zhang Xianliang

No emperor has the power to dictate to the heart.
Johann Friedrich Von Schiller

The sole advantage of power is that you can do more good.
Baltasar Gracián

There are two ways of exerting one's strength: One is pushing down, the other is pulling up.
Booker T. Washington

Power is no blessing in itself, except when it is used to protect the innocent.
Jonathan Swift

We have, I fear, confused power with greatness.
Stewart Udall

Problems and Solutions

The problem when solved will be simple.
Sign on the wall of a General Motors research laboratory

When the solution is simple, God is answering.
Albert Einstein

All things are difficult before they are easy.
Dr. Thomas Fuller

I have learned to use the word impossible with the greatest caution.
Wernher Von Braun

If you think the problem is bad now, just wait until we've solved it.
Arthur Kasspe

Never cut what you can untie.
Joseph Joubert

It's not that I'm so smart. It's just that I stay with problems longer.
Albert Einstein

No problem can stand the assault of sustained thinking.
Voltaire

No problem is so formidable that you can't walk away from it.
Charles Schulz

A clever person solves a problem. A wise person avoids it.
Albert Einstein

Ideas may also grow out of the problem itself, which in turn becomes part of the solution.
Paul Rand

Never state a problem to yourself in the same terms it was brought to you.
Wendell Castle

A problem well stated is a problem half solved.
Charles F. Kettering

Every problem contains within itself the seeds of its own solution.
Stanley Arnold

The greatest challenge to any thinker is stating the problem in a way that will allow a solution.
Bertrand Russell

An undefined problem has an infinite number of solutions.
Robert A. Humphrey

The way we see the problem is the problem.
Stephen R. Covey

It's not easy taking my problems one at a time when they refuse to get in line.
Ashleigh Brilliant

The solution of every problem is another problem.
Johann Wolfgang von Goethe

Each success only buys an admission ticket to a more difficult problem.
Henry Kissinger

Two paradoxes are better than one; they may even suggest a solution.
> Edward Teller

I don't have any solution, but I certainly admire the problem.
> Ashleigh Brilliant

The greatest and most important problems of life are all fundamentally insoluble. They can never be solved but only outgrown.
> Carl Jung

Too often we give children answers to remember rather than problems to solve.
> Roger Lewin

The problem is not that there are problems. The problem is expecting otherwise and thinking that having problems is a problem.
> Theodore Isaac Rubin

All problems become smaller if you don't dodge them but confront them.
> William F. Halsey

Problems worthy of attack prove their worth by hitting back.
> Piet Hein

Every human being is a problem in search of a solution.
> Ashley Montagu

The significant problems we face cannot be solved at the same level of thinking we were at when we created them.
> Albert Einstein

For every complex problem, there is a solution that is simple, neat, and wrong.
> H.L. Mencken

If you think there is a solution, you are part of the problem.
> George Carlin

It isn't that they can't see the solution. It is that they can't see the problem.
> G.K. Chesterton

You're either part of the problem or part of the solution.
> Eldridge Cleaver

Problems are only opportunities in work clothes.
> Henry John Kaiser

Every problem has a gift for you in its hands.
> Richard Bache

Progress

Progress might have been all right once but it has gone on too long.
Ogden Nash

Is it progress if a cannibal uses a knife and fork?
Stanislaw J. Lec

People who don't believe in progress must have forgotten how bad things used to be.
Ashleigh Brilliant

The art of progress is to preserve order amid change, and to preserve change amid order. Life refuses to be embalmed alive.
Alfred North Whitehead

I was taught that the way of progress is neither swift nor easy.
Marie Curie

What we call progress is the exchange of one nuisance for another nuisance.
Henry Havelock Ellis

The magnitude of a "progress" is gauged by the sacrifice that it requires.
Friedrich Nietzsche

The criterion of "progress" between two cultures or two eras consists of a greater capacity to kill.
Nicolás Gómez-Dávila

You can't say civilizations don't advance. In every war they kill you in a new way.
Will Rogers

You can't sit on the lid of progress. If you do, you will be blown to pieces.
Henry John Kaiser

Progress is impossible without change, and those who cannot change their minds cannot change anything.
George Bernard Shaw

How wonderful that we have met with a paradox. Now we have some hope of making progress.
Niels Bohr

Whatever there be of progress in life comes not through adaptation but through daring, through the blind urge.
Henry Miller

All progress is based upon a universal innate desire of every organism to live beyond its means.
    Samuel Butler

Progress is man's ability to complicate simplicity.
    Thor Heyerdahl

A lot of what appears to be progress is just so much technological rococo.
    Bill Gray

There can be no progress if people have no faith in tomorrow.
    John F. Kennedy

Progress might be a circle, rather than a straight line.
    Eberhard Zeidler

Man's progress is but a gradual discovery that his questions have no meaning.
    Antoine de Saint-Exupéry

Progress is a comfortable disease.
    e.e. cummings

Progress is made by lazy men looking for easier ways to do things.
    Robert Heinlein

Man is in danger of being made obsolete by his own progress.
    Burton Hillis

The reasonable man adapts himself to the world; the unreasonable man persists in trying to adapt the world to himself. Therefore, all progress depends on the unreasonable man.
    George Bernard Shaw

There are many ways of going forward, but only one way of standing still.
    Franklin D. Roosevelt

Progress lies not in embracing what is, but in advancing toward what will be.
    Kahlil Gibran

People fascinated by the idea of progress never suspect that every step forward is also a step on the way to the end.
    Milan Kundera

All progress has resulted from people who took unpopular positions.
    Adlai Stevenson

Discontent is the first step in the progress of a man or a nation.
    Oscar Wilde

Every great advance in natural knowledge has involved the absolute rejection of authority.
Thomas Henry Huxley

Human progress is furthered, not by conformity, but by aberration.
H.L. Mencken

Without deviation, progress is not possible.
Frank Zappa

Questions and Answers

It is not the answer that enlightens, but the question.
Eugène Ionesco

Putting a question correctly is one thing and finding the answer to it is something quite different.
Anton Chekhov

My whole life is waiting for the questions to which I have prepared answers.
Tom Stoppard

He who asks questions cannot avoid the answers.
Cameroon Proverb

The only questions worth asking today are whether humans are going to have any emotions tomorrow, and what the quality of life will be if the answer is no.
Lester Bangs

If they can get you asking the wrong questions, they don't have to worry about the answers.
Thomas Pynchon

The important thing is not to stop questioning.
Albert Einstein

Question everything.
Georg Christoph Lichtenberg

Every sentence that I utter must be understood not as an affirmation, but as a question.
Niels Bohr

It is a good answer which knows when to stop.
Italian Proverb

To ask the hard question is simple.
> W.H. Auden

I don't pretend we have all the answers. But the questions are certainly worth thinking about.
> Arthur C. Clarke

It is better to debate a question without settling it than to settle a question without debating it.
> Joseph Joubert

Judge a man by his questions rather than by his answers.
> Voltaire

You can tell whether a man is clever by his answers. You can tell whether a man is wise by his questions.
> Mahfouz Naguib

Good questions outrank easy answers.
> Paul Anthony Samuelson

Never answer a hypothetical question.
> Moshe Arens

Freedom from the desire for an answer is essential to the understanding of a problem.
> Jiddu Krishnamurti

Some questions don't have answers, which is a terribly difficult lesson to learn.
> Katharine Graham

No answer is also an answer
> German Proverb

The shortest answer is doing.
> English Proverb

Questions are never indiscreet. Answers sometimes are.
> Oscar Wilde

There aren't any embarrassing questions – only embarrassing answers.
> Carl Rowan

No man really becomes a fool until he stops asking questions.
> Charles Proteus Steinmetz

The "silly" question is the first intimation of some totally new development.
> Alfred North Whitehead

He who asks a question is a fool for five minutes; he who does not ask a question remains a fool forever.
>Chinese Proverb

The job is to ask questions – it always was – and to ask them as inexorably as I can. And to face the absence of precise answers with a certain humility.
>Arthur Miller

It is better to know some of the questions than all the answers.
>James Thurber

It is not every question that deserves an answer.
>Publilius Syrus

Einstein was a man who could ask immensely simple questions. And what his work showed is that when the answers are simple too, then you can hear God thinking.
>Jacob Bronowski

Live the questions now.
>Rainer Maria Rilke

A wise man's question contains half the answer.
>Solomon Ibn Gabirol

Be patient toward all that is unsolved in your heart and try to love the questions themselves like locked rooms and like books that are written in a very foreign tongue.
>Rainer Maria Rilke

The only interesting answers are those that destroy the questions.
>Susan Sontag

Only a weak mind seeks ultimate answers.
>Agnes Thornton

The ultimate answers cannot be given, they can only be received.
>Tom Robbins

Reality

Reality is nothing but a collective hunch.
    Lily Tomlin

Nothing exists except atoms and empty space; everything else is opinion.
    Democritus

All our separate fictions add up to joint reality.
    Stanislaw J. Lec

For what we regard as reality is conditioned by the theory to which we subscribe.
    Stephen Hawking

We must select the illusion which appeals to our temperament and embrace it with passion.
    Cyril Connolly

Reality is merely an illusion, albeit a very persistent one
    Albert Einstein

Reality is that which, when you stop believing in it, doesn't go away.
    Philip K. Dick

Reality is still the only place to get a good steak.
    Woody Allen

I believe in looking reality straight in the eye and denying it.
    Garrison Keillor

Reality continues to ruin my life.
    Bill Watterson

No doubt the world is entirely an imaginary world, but it is only once removed from the real world.
    Isaac Bashevis Singer

Things are not as they seem to be, yet they are not otherwise.
    Lankavatara Sutra

Since we cannot change reality, let us change the eyes which see reality.
    Nikos Kazantzakis

Use your mentality, Wake up to reality.
    Cole Porter

Reality, what a concept.
    Robin Williams

Now, my own suspicion is that the universe is not only queerer than we suppose, but queerer than we *can* suppose.
 J.B.S. Haldane

Any experience of reality is indescribable!
 R.D. Laing

Are you really sure that a floor can't also be a ceiling?
 M.C. Escher

Nothing is what it seems.
 Jim Thompson

Words, as is well known, are the great foes of reality.
 Joseph Conrad

Human kind cannot bear much reality.
 T. S. Eliot

Reality leaves a lot to the imagination.
 John Lennon

Reality is something you rise above.
 Liza Minnelli

Everything you can imagine is real.
 Pablo Picasso

Reality only reveals itself when it is illuminated by a ray of poetry.
 Georges Braque

Few people have the imagination for reality.
 Johann Wolfgang von Goethe

Reality is the cage of those who lack imagination.
 J.B.S. Haldane

The dignity of man lies in his ability to face reality in all its meaninglessness.
 Martin Esslin

I like reality. It tastes of bread.
 Jean Anouilh

Rebellion and Revolution

A little rebellion now and then is a good thing.
> Thomas Jefferson

Every act of rebellion expresses a nostalgia for innocence and an appeal to the essence of being.
> Albert Camus

Most people have a natural instinct to rebel.
> Elvis Presley

The revolution was effected before the war even commenced. The revolution was in the hearts and minds of the people.
> John Adams, on the American Revolution

Be not deceived. Revolutions do not go backward.
> Abraham Lincoln

Until they become conscious they will never rebel, and until they have rebelled they cannot become conscious.
> George Orwell

Bring the War Home.
> Slogan of the Weather Underground

The first duty of a revolutionary is to get away with it.
> Abbie Hoffman

The most radical revolutionary will become a conservative the day after the revolution.
> Hannah Arendt

A true revolutionary is guided by a great feeling of love.
> Ernesto Che Guevara

The purity of a revolution can last a fortnight.
> Jean Cocteau

Revolution is a trivial shift in the emphasis of suffering.
> Tom Stoppard

In the fight between you and the world, back the world.
> Frank Zappa

No one can go on being a rebel too long without turning into an autocrat.
> Lawrence Durrell

Every revolutionary ends as an oppressor or a heretic.
Albert Camus

Rebel, n. A proponent of a new misrule who has failed to establish it.
Ambrose Bierce, The Devil's Dictionary

We started off trying to set up a small anarchist community, but people wouldn't obey the rules.
Alan Bennett

The moment you have a plan you cease to be a revolutionary.
Daniel Cohn-Bendit

The revolution will not be televised
The revolution will be no re-run brothers
The revolution will be live.
Gil Scott-Heron

What is a rebel? A man who says no.
Albert Camus

Whatever it is I'm against it.
Groucho Marx

If you're going to kick authority in the teeth, you might as well use two feet.
Keith Richards

As a dimension of man, rebellion actually defines him.
Robert Lindner

Every normal man must be tempted, at times, to spit on his hands, hoist the black flag, and begin slitting throats.
H.L. Mencken

When I hear the word "culture", I reach for my gun.
Hans Johst

The end move in politics is always to pick up a gun.
R. Buckminster Fuller

If there is a gun hanging on the wall in the first act, it must fire in the last.
Anton Chekhov, advice to a novice playwright

If we make peaceful revolution impossible, we make violent revolution inevitable.
John F. Kennedy

It's too soon to tell.
>   Ho Chi Minh, when asked if the French Revolution made a difference

Rebellion without truth is like spring in a bleak, arid desert.
>   Kahlil Gibran

When smashing monuments, save the pedestals – they always come in handy.
>   Stanislaw Lem

Whaddya got?
>   Marlon Brando in The Wild One, when asked
>   "What are you rebelling against, Johnny?"

Religion

Every day people are straying away from church and going back to God.
>   Lenny Bruce

Religion is what happens when God has left the building.
>   Bono

I like the silent church before the service begins, better than any preaching.
>   Ralph Waldo Emerson

Don't pray when it rains if you don't pray when the sun shines.
>   Leroy (Satchel) Paige

The more I study religions the more I am convinced that man never worshipped anything but himself.
>   Sir Richard Francis Burton

People who want to share their religious views with you almost never want you to share yours with them.
>   Dave Barry

The best religion is tolerance.
>   Victor Hugo

The greatest tragedy in mankind's entire history may be the hijacking of morality by religion.
>   Arthur C. Clarke

Of all the tyrannies that affect mankind, tyranny in religion is the worst.
>   Thomas Paine

Man's uneasiness is such, that the vagueness and the mystery which religion presents are absolutely necessary to him.
> Napoleon Bonaparte

Randomness scares people. Religion is a way to explain randomness.
> Fran Lebowitz

When people are least sure, they are often most dogmatic.
> John Kenneth Galbraith

Religion is a magic device for turning unanswerable questions into unquestionable answers.
> Art Gecko

Religion is the love of life in the consciousness of impotence.
> George Santayana

Religion is a disease, but it is a noble disease.
> Heraclitus

Religion is a bandage that man has invented to protect a soul made bloody by circumstance.
> Theodore Dreiser

Religion is what keeps the poor from murdering the rich.
> Napoleon Bonaparte

We have just enough religion to make us hate, but not enough to make us love one another.
> Jonathan Swift

Nature teaches us to love our friends, but religion our enemies.
> Dr. Thomas Fuller

Nothing frightens me more than religion at my door.
> John Cale

I've got enough guilt to start my own religion.
> Tori Amos

Writing for a penny a word is ridiculous. If a man really wants to make a million dollars, the best way would be to start his own religion.
> L. Ronald Hubbard

It is the test of a good religion whether you can make a joke about it.
> G.K. Chesterton

Religion is by no means a proper subject of conversation in mixed company.
Lord Chesterfield

Religion is the fashionable substitute for belief.
Oscar Wilde

Children are naive – they trust everyone. School is bad enough, but, if you put a child anywhere in the vicinity of a church, you're asking for trouble.
Frank Zappa

I hope I never get so old I get religious.
Ingmar Bergman

My religion consists of a humble admiration of the illimitable superior spirit who reveals himself in the slight details we are able to perceive with our frail and feeble minds.
Albert Einstein

My religion is simple. My religion is kindness.
Tenzin Gyatso, 14th Dalai Lama

My country is the world, and my religion is to do good.
Thomas Paine

When I do good, I feel good. When I do bad, I feel bad. That's my religion.
Abraham Lincoln

Every religion is good that teaches man to be good.
Thomas Paine

One's religion is whatever he is most interested in.
Sir James M. Barrie

True religion is the life we lead, not the creed we profess.
Louis Nizer

Where true religion has prevented one crime, false religions have afforded a pretext for a thousand.
Charles Caleb Colton

Men never do evil so completely and cheerfully as when they do it from religious convictions.
Blaise Pascal

Nothing is so fatal to religion as indifference.
Edmund Burke

An old argument with me is that the true religious force in the world is not the church but the world itself.
Wallace Stevens

Science without religion is lame; religion without science is blind.
Albert Einstein

Religion is the highest vanity.
Friedrich Hebbel

I am an atheist still, thank God.
Luis Buñuel

I'm a born again atheist.
Gore Vidal

It's the priests who have demands, not the gods.
Stanislaw J. Lec

Knowledge and history are the enemies of religion.
Napoleon Bonaparte

One who recovers from sickness forgets about God.
Ethiopian Proverb

In prosperity no altars smoke.
Italian Proverb

The whole purpose of religion is to facilitate love and compassion, patience, tolerance, humility, and forgiveness.
Tenzin Gyatso, 14th Dalai Lama

To die for a religion is easier than to live it absolutely.
Jorge Luis Borges

Religion is a candle inside a multicolored lantern. Everyone looks through a particular color, but the candle is always there.
Mohammed Naguib

There is only one religion, though there are a hundred versions of it.
George Bernard Shaw

I have always respected everyone's religion. As I say, there is only one God and a lot of confused people.
Hazel Scott

God has no religion.
      Mahatma Gandhi

Say nothing of my religion. It is known to God and myself alone.
      Thomas Jefferson

Religion is excellent stuff for keeping common people quite.
      Napoleon Bonaparte

Religion...is the opium of the people.
      Karl Marx

I'm looking of loopholes.
      W.C. Fields, explaining why he was reading a Bible

Sanity and Madness

The only difference between me and a madman is that I am not mad.
      Salvador Dali

There is a pleasure sure, in being mad which none but madmen know.
      John Dryden

It is much more comfortable to be mad and know it, than to be sane and have
one's doubts.
      GB Burgin

A man who is "of sound mind" is one who keeps the inner madman under lock
and key.
      Paul Valéry

Most men are within a finger's breadth of being mad.
      Diogenes

You're only given a little spark of madness. You mustn't lose it.
      Robin Williams

Insanity is a kind of innocence.
      Graham Greene

The perfection of innocence, indeed, is madness.
      Arthur Miller

A man needs a little madness or else he never dares to cut the rope and be free.
      Anthony Quinn, Zorba the Greek

When we remember we are all mad, the mysteries disappear and life stands explained.
        Mark Twain

Sanity is a madness put to good uses; waking life is a dream controlled.
        George Santayana

When the going gets weird, the weird turn pro.
        Hunter S. Thompson

I saw the best minds of my generation destroyed by madness, starving hysterical naked, dragging themselves through the negro streets at dawn looking for an angry fix…
        Allen Ginsberg

That is the truest sign of insanity – insane people are always sure that they are fine. It is only the sane people who are willing to admit that they are crazy.
        Nora Ephron

Sanity is a cozy lie.
        Susan Sontag

Those who dance are considered insane by those who can't hear the music.
        George Carlin

No sane man will dance.
        Marcus Tullius Cicero

Sanity calms, but madness is more interesting.
        Lord John Russell

Not every kind of madness is a calamity.
        Desiderius Erasmus

The extreme limit of wisdom, that's what the public calls madness.
        Jean Cocteau

Truly great madness can not be achieved without significant intelligence.
        Henrik Tikkanen

Though this be madness, yet there is method in't.
        William Shakespeare

The only people for me are the mad ones, the ones who are mad to live, mad to talk, desirous of everything at the same time.
        Jack Kerouac

Madness is to think of too many things in succession too fast or of one thing too exclusively.
Voltaire

Insanity is often the logic of an accurate mind overtasked.
Oliver Wendell Holmes

I've always been crazy, but it's kept me from going insane.
Waylon Jennings

Of all the things I've ever lost I miss my mind the most.
Steven Tyler

We all agree that your theory is crazy, but is it crazy enough?
Niels Bohr

We do not have to visit a madhouse to find disordered minds; our planet is the mental institution of the universe.
Johann Wolfgang von Goethe

Madness is rare in individuals – but in groups, political parties, nations, and eras it's the rule.
Friedrich Nietzsche

Sanity is only the madness preferred by the majority.
Kevin Blonske

Once upon a time crazy meant something, now everyone's crazy.
Charles Manson

Insanity – a perfectly rational adjustment to an insane world.
R.D. Laing

Where does one go from a world of insanity? Somewhere on the other side of despair.
T.S. Eliot

What sane person could live in this world and not be crazy?
Ursula K. Le Guin

In a mad world, only the mad are sane.
Akiro Kurosawa

Anyone who goes to a psychiatrist ought to have his head examined.
Samuel Goldwyn, attributed

When dealing with the insane, the best method is to pretend to be sane.
Hermann Hesse

Ordinarily he is insane. But he has lucid moments when he is only stupid.
Heinrich Heine

I became insane… with intervals of horrible sanity.
Edgar Allan Poe

I read somewhere that 77 percent of all the mentally ill live in poverty. Actually, I'm more intrigued by the 23 percent who are apparently doing quite well for themselves.
Emo Phillips

Show me a sane man and I will cure him for you.
Carl Gustav Jung

Self-Esteem

Nobody holds a good opinion of a man who has a low opinion of himself.
Anthony Trollope

I've been dirt, and I don't care.
Iggy Pop

Low self-esteem is like driving through life with your hand-break on.
Maxwell Maltz

Of all our infirmities, the most savage is to despise our being.
Michel de Montaigne

I feel stupid and contagious.
Kurt Cobain

He who knows himself best, esteems himself least.
Proverb

Perhaps the only true dignity of man is his capacity to despise himself.
George Santayana

He that undervalues himself will undervalue others, and he that undervalues others will oppress them.
Samuel Johnson

The person we believe ourselves to be will always act in a manner consistent with our self-image.
Brian Tracy

To love oneself is the beginning of a lifelong romance.
Oscar Wilde

I never loved another person the way I loved myself.
  Mae West

Love yourself first and everything else falls into line.
  Lucille Ball

A narcissist is someone better looking than you are.
  Gore Vidal

Lots of real creeps have self-respect. They just have a creepy version of it.
  Robert B. Parker

We are valued in this world at the rate we desire to be valued.
  Jean de La Bruyère

Respect yourself if you would have others respect you.
  Baltasar Gracián

So much is a man worth as he esteems himself.
  Francois Rabelais

All the extraordinary men I have known were extraordinary in their own estimation.
  Woodrow Wilson

A man cannot be comfortable without his own approval.
  Mark Twain

No one can make you feel inferior without your consent.
  Eleanor Roosevelt

We are all primary numbers divisible only by ourselves.
  Jean Guitton

It's hard to fight an enemy who has outposts in your head.
  Sally Kempton

When there is no enemy within, the enemies outside cannot hurt you.
  African Proverb

Self-confidence is the first requisite to great undertakings.
  Samuel Johnson

The greatest success, is successful self-acceptance.
  Ben Sweet

Self-Realization

We are all of us in the gutter. But some of us are looking at the stars.
    Oscar Wilde

The man in the street does not know a star in the sky.
    Ralph Waldo Emerson

We all live under the same sky, but we don't have the same horizon.
    Konrad Adenauer

Our aspirations are our possibilities.
    Samuel Johnson

Who are we, not to shine?
    Nelson Mandela

We know what we are, but know not what we may be.
    William Shakespeare

To be what we are, and to become what we are capable of becoming, is the only end of life.
    Robert Louis Stevenson

First say to yourself what you would be; and then do what you have to do.
    Epictetus

Thoroughly to know oneself, is above all art, for it is the highest art.
    Theologia Germanica

Know thyself? If I knew myself, I'd run away.
    Johann Wolfgang von Goethe

Be yourself. Everyone else is already taken.
    Gilbert Perreira

Any life... is made up of a single moment – the moment in which a man finds out, once and for all, who he is.
    Jorge Luis Borges

As human beings, our greatness lies not so much in being able to remake the world as in being able to remake ourselves.
    Mahatma Gandhi

Love not what you are, but what you may become.
    Miguel de Cervantes

It is never too late to be what you might have been.
George Eliot

Nothing ever is, everything is becoming.
Plato

When we strive to become better than we are, everything around us becomes better, too.
Paulo Coelho

Self-knowledge and self-improvement are very difficult for most people. It usually needs great courage and long struggle.
Abraham H. Maslow

I know who I am and who I may be, if I choose.
Miguel de Cervantes

It takes courage to grow up and become who you really are.
e.e. cummings

What shall it profit a man, if he shall gain the whole world, and lose his own soul?
Bible, Mark 8:36

Don't compromise yourself. You're all you've got.
Janis Joplin

To find yourself you need the greatest possible freedom to drift.
Francis Bacon

Conquer yourself not the world.
René Descartes

The power of man has grown in every sphere, except over himself.
Winston Churchill

The greatest of victories is the victory over oneself.
The Dhammapada

It is not the mountain we conquer but ourselves.
Edmund Hillary

We have met the enemy and he is us.
Walt Kelly

My life is like one long obstacle course with me being the obstacle.
Jack Paar

We meet ourselves time and again in a thousand disguises on the path of life.
> Carl Gustav Jung

Our goal is to discover that we have always been where we ought to be.
> Aldous Huxley

Enlarge your consciousness. If your consciousness is small, you will experience smallness in every department of your life.
> Robert Pante

One may understand the cosmos, but never the ego; the self is more distant than any star.
> G.K. Chesterton

We are what we repeatedly do.
> Aristotle

I always wanted to be somebody, but I should have been more specific.
> Lily Tomlin

Everybody wants to be somebody; nobody wants to grow.
> Johann Wolfgang von Goethe

We are what we pretend to be, so we must be careful about what we pretend to be.
> Kurt Vonnegut

He who knows others is wise; he who knows himself is enlightened.
> Lao-Tzu

Everyone thinks of changing humanity; no one thinks of changing himself.
> Leo Tolstoy

The life that is not examined is not worth living.
> Plato

You must imagine your life, and then it happens.
> John Updike

If you cannot be a poet, be the poem.
> David Carradine

Take what you can use and let the rest go by.
> Ken Kesey

Fundamentalists believe Jesus was God becoming man. I believe that Jesus was man becoming God.
> Eric Butterworth

Don't be afraid to go out on a limb. That's where the fruit is.
Arthur F. Lenehan

Never saw off the branch you are on, unless you are being hanged from it.
Stanislaw J. Lec

What lies behind us and what lies before us are tiny matters compared to what lies within us.
Ralph Waldo Emerson

We dig within in order to go beyond.
Ken Wilber

I am always doing that which I can not do, in order that I may learn how to do it.
Pablo Picasso

It's kind of fun to do the impossible.
Walt Disney

But the only way of discovering the limits of the possible is to venture a little way past them into the impossible.
Arthur C. Clarke

When I let go of what I am, I become what I might be.
Lao-Tzu

Man's main task in life is to give birth to himself.
Erich Fromm

He not busy being born is busy dying.
Bob Dylan

The strongest principle of growth lies in the human choice.
George Eliot

Your sole contribution to the sum of things is yourself.
Frank Crane

Sex

Sex without love is an empty experience, but, as empty experiences go, it's one of the best.
> Woody Allen

Sex without love is merely healthy exercise
> Robert Heinlein

Sex is the biggest nothing of our time.
> Andy Warhol

Sex: the thing that takes up the least amount of time and causes the most amount of trouble.
> John Barrymore

What urge will save us now that sex won't?
> Jenny Holzer

If your sexual fantasies were truly of interest to others, they would no longer be fantasies.
> Fran Lebowitz

Sex appeal is fifty per cent what you've got, and fifty per cent what people think you've got.
> Sophia Loren

The mind can also be an erogenous zone.
> Raquel Welch

When authorities warn you of the sinfulness of sex, there is an important lesson to be learned. Do not have sex with the authorities.
> Matt Groening

If sex is such a natural phenomenon, how come there are so many books on how to do it?
> Bette Midler

Why should we take advice on sex from the Pope. If he knows anything, he shouldn't.
> George Bernard Shaw

Personally, I know nothing about sex, because I've always been married.
> Zsa Zsa Gabor

Of all the sexual aberrations, perhaps the most peculiar is chastity.
> Rémy de Gourmont

I believe that sex is one of the most beautiful, natural, wholesome things that money can buy.
Steve Martin

If it weren't for pickpockets, I'd have no sex life at all.
Rodney Dangerfield

Sex should be friendly. Otherwise stick to mechanical toys; it's more sanitary.
Robert Heinlein

The only unnatural sex act is one which you cannot perform.
Alfred Kinsey

Does it really matter what these affectionate people do – so long as they don't do it in the streets and frighten the horses!
Beatrice Campbell

Sex is one of the nine reasons for reincarnation. The other eight are unimportant.
Henry Miller

Silence

Silence is also speech.
West African Proverb

Silence is the only language we all speak.
Brett Banfe

Silence is argument carried out by other means.
Ernesto Che Guevara

Silence may be as variously shaded as speech.
Edith Wharton

Silence is a text easy to misread.
A.A. Attanasio

Silence is one of the hardest arguments to refute.
Josh Billings

I have often regretted my speech, never my silence.
Publilius Syrus

If a thing goes without saying – let it.
Jacob M. Braude

Blessed is the man, who having nothing to say, abstains from giving wordy evidence of the fact.
George Eliot

It is as important to cultivate your silence power as it is your word power.
William James

In human intercourse the tragedy begins, not when there is misunderstanding about words, but when silence is not understood.
Henry David Thoreau

Silence is a true friend who never betrays.
Confucius

Speech is of time, silence is of eternity.
Thomas Carlyle

Do not the most moving moments of our lives find us all without words?
Marcel Marceau

He has occasional flashes of silence, that make his conversation perfectly delightful.
Sydney Smith

'Tis easier to know how to speak than how to be silent.
Dr. Thomas Fuller

An inability to stay quiet is one of the most conspicuous failings of mankind.
Walter Bagehot

The right word may be effective, but no word was ever as effective as a rightly timed pause.
Mark Twain

Every word is like an unnecessary stain on silence and nothingness.
Samuel Beckett

Men fear silence as they fear solitude, because both give them a glimpse of the terror of life's nothingness.
André Maurois

It's good to shut up sometimes.
Marcel Marceau

The silent dog is the first to bite.
German Proverb

Nothing strengthens authority so much as silence.
Charles de Gaulle

Silence is the language of God; It is also the language of the heart.
   Dag Hammerskjöld

Let us be silent, that we may hear the whispers of the gods.
   Ralph Waldo Emerson

The quieter you become the more you can hear.
   Baba Ram Dass

When you are climbing a mountain, don't talk; silence gives ascent.
   Robert J. Burdette

Nothing is more useful than silence.
   Menander

The temple of our purest thoughts is silence.
   Sarah J. Hale

There are very few people who do not become more interesting when they stop talking.
   Mary Lowry

A man is known by the silence he keeps.
   Oliver Herford

Do you wish people to believe good of you? Don't speak.
   Blaise Pascal

Let a fool hold his tongue and he will pass for a sage.
   Publilius Syrus

Who knows most says least.
   Spanish Proverb

No wisdom like silence.
   Chinese Proverb

Silence is true wisdom's best reply.
   Euripides

Silence is the element in which great things fashion themselves together.
   Thomas Carlyle

Silence is man's chief learning.
   Palladas

Don't speak unless you can improve on the silence.
   Spanish Proverb

Sometimes you have to be silent to be heard
    Stanislaw J. Lec

Who the hell wants to hear actors talk?
    H.M. Warner, Warner Brothers, 1927

Never get a mime talking. He won't stop.
    Marcel Marceau

Sin

All sins are attempts to fill voids.
    Simone Weil

Sin is whatever obscures the soul.
    André Gide

The world is as ugly as sin, and almost as delightful.
    Frederick Locker-Lampson

We cannot well do without our sins; they are the highway of our virtue.
    Henry David Thoreau

The only difference between the saint and the sinner is that every saint has a past, and every sinner has a future.
    Oscar Wilde

Saints are sinners who kept on going.
    Robert Louis Stevenson

Sins cannot be undone, only forgiven.
    Igor Stravinsky

Once a woman has forgiven her man, she must not reheat his sins for breakfast.
    Marlene Dietrich

A sin confessed is half forgiven.
    French Proverb

The sinning is the best part of repentance.
    Arab Proverb

There is a charm about the forbidden that makes it unspeakably desirable.
    Mark Twain

Lead me not into temptation; I can find the way myself.
Rita Mae Brown

Without a spice of guilt, sin cannot be fully savored.
Alexander Chase

If it were possible to have a life absolutely free from every feeling of sin, what a terrifying vacuum it would be!
Cesare Pavese

Hate the sin and love the sinner.
Mahatma Gandhi

You don't make up for your sins in church. You do it at home and you do it in the streets. And the rest is bullshit and you know that.
Martin Scorsese

Jesus died for somebody's sins but not mine.
Patti Smith

Christ died for our sins. Dare we make his martyrdom meaningless by not committing them.
Jules Feiffer

We are punished by our sins, not for them.
Elbert G. Hubbard

The major sin is the sin of being born.
Samuel Beckett

Really to sin you have to be serious about it.
Henrik Ibsen

Many are saved from sin by being so inept at it.
Mignon McLaughlin

There is no sin except stupidity.
Oscar Wilde

Pleasure's a sin and sometimes sin's a pleasure.
Lord Byron

Sin is geographical.
Bertrand Russell

That which we call sin in others is experiment for us.
Ralph Waldo Emerson

No one ever suddenly became depraved.
Juvenal

Sins become more subtle as you grow older: you commit sins of despair rather than lust.
Piers Paul Read

A man does not sin by commission only, but often by omission.
Marcus Aurelius

There's no such thing as an original sin.
Elvis Costello

Spirit

We are not human beings on a spiritual journey. We are spiritual beings on a human journey.
Stephen R. Covey

The foundations of a person are not in matter but in spirit.
Ralph Waldo Emerson

I feel within me that spark, that atom emanation of the divine spirit.
Giuseppe Verdi

Firmament and planets both disappeared, but the mighty breath which gives life to all things and in which all is bound up remained.
Vincent Van Gogh, describing his painting Starry Night

I simply believe that some part of the human soul is not subject to the laws of space and time.
Carl Gustav Jung

The spirit down here in man and the spirit up there in the sun, in reality are only one spirit, and there is no other one.
The Upanishads

Lift the stone and you will find me; cleave the wood and I am there.
Jesus Christ, The Gospel of Thomas

The life of the spirit is not our life, but the life of God within us.
Saint Teresa of Avila

The more I study physics, the more I am drawn to metaphysics.
Albert Einstein

Pure logic is the ruin of the spirit.
>Antoine de Saint-Exupéry

The Spirit's foe in man has not been simplicity, but sophistication.
>George Santayana

Physical strength can never permanently withstand the impact of spiritual force.
>Franklin D. Roosevelt

Great spirits have always encountered violent opposition from mediocre minds.
>Albert Einstein

I am certainly convinced that it is one of the greatest impulses of mankind to arrive at something higher than a natural state.
>James Baldwin

Everyone who is seriously involved in the pursuit of science becomes convinced that a Spirit is manifest in the laws of the Universe.
>Albert Einstein

Without the spiritual world the material world is a disheartening enigma.
>Joseph Joubert

The sword conquered for a while, but the spirit conquers forever!
>Sholem Asch

In loving the spiritual, you cannot despise the earthly.
>Joseph Campbell

The spirit of man is an inward flame; a lamp the world blows upon but never puts out.
>Margot Asquith

The spirit illuminates everything.
>Chinese Proverb

More light!
>Last words of Johann Wolfgang von Goethe

There is a light that never goes out.
>Morrissey

Success

Eighty percent of success is showing up.
> Woody Allen

There is only one success. To be able to spend life in your own way.
> Christopher Morley

If your success is not on your own terms, if it looks good to the world but does not feel good in your heart, it is not success at all.
> Anna Quindlen

Success is relative: it is what we can make of the mess we have made of things.
> T.S. Eliot

The road to success is always under construction.
> Arnold Palmer

Success is never final.
> Winston Churchill

There is no point at which you can say, "Well, I'm successful now. I might as well take a nap."
> Carrie Fisher

The toughest thing about success is that you've got to keep on being a success.
> Irving Berlin

Is there anything in life so disenchanting as attainment?
> Robert Louis Stevenson

I dread success. To have succeeded is to have finished one's business on earth. I like a state of continual becoming, with a goal in front and not behind.
> George Bernard Shaw

The worst part of success is trying to find someone who is happy for you.
> Bette Midler

The only way to succeed is to make people hate you.
> Josef Von Sternberg

Success is the one unpardonable sin against one's fellows.
> Ambrose Bierce

Pray that success will not come any faster than you are able to endure it.
> Elbert G. Hubbard

Success didn't spoil me. I've always been insufferable.
    Fran Lebowitz

Nothing makes a man so cross as success.
    Anthony Trollope

Every man has the right to be conceited until he is successful.
    Benjamin Disraeli

Sometimes I worry about being a success in a mediocre world.
    Lily Tomlin

Try not to become a man of success, but rather try to become a man of value.
    Albert Einstein

The secret to success is sincerity. Once you can fake that, you've got it made.
    Jean Giraudoux

Nothing succeeds like the appearance of success.
    Christopher Lasch

Success has made failures of many men.
    Cindy Adams

Nothing is more humiliating than to see idiots succeed in enterprises we have failed in.
    Gustave Flaubert

Success in almost any field depends more on energy and drive than it does on intelligence. This explains why we have so many stupid leaders.
    Sloan Wilson

To succeed in the world it is not enough to be stupid, you must also be well-mannered.
    Voltaire

All you need in this life is ignorance and confidence, and then success is sure.
    Mark Twain

Success has always been a great liar.
    Friedrich Nietzsche

Success is a great deodorant.
    Elizabeth Taylor

It is not enough to succeed. Others must fail.
    Gore Vidal

Nothing recedes like success.
Walter Winchell

Success generally depends upon knowing how long it takes to succeed.
Baron de Montesquieu

The secret of success is consistency of purpose.
Benjamin Disraeli

The secret of success is this: there is no secret of success.
Elbert G. Hubbard

The most important single ingredient in the formula of success is knowing how to get along with people.
Theodore Roosevelt

Success seems to be largely a matter of hanging on after others have let go.
William Feather

Success is the ability to go from failure to failure without losing your enthusiasm.
Winston Churchill

Success is how high you bounce when you hit bottom.
George S. Patton

Success does not consist in never making mistakes but in never making the same one a second time.
George Bernard Shaw

Failure is success if we learn from it.
Malcolm Forbes

If at first you don't succeed try, try again. Then quit. No use being a damn fool about it.
W.C. Fields

If at first you do succeed – try to hide your astonishment.
Harry F. Banks

Success is simply a matter of luck. Ask any failure.
Earl Wilson

Success can eliminate as many options as failure.
Tom Robbins

Success and failure are equally disastrous.
Tennessee Williams

About the only problem with success is that it does not teach you how to deal with failure.
Tommy Lasorda

Those who have succeeded at anything and don't mention luck are kidding themselves.
Larry King

Put your heart, mind, intellect and soul even to your smallest acts. This is the secret of success.
Sri Swami Sivananda

A man can succeed at almost anything for which he has unlimited enthusiasm.
Charles Schwab

You never achieve real success unless you like what you are doing.
Dale Carnegie

Success comes to those who dare and act, it seldom goes to timid.
Jawaharlal Nehru

It never fails. Everybody who really makes it does it by busting his ass.
Alan Arkin

Success is not the result of spontaneous combustion. You must set yourself on fire.
Reggie Leach

Some succeed because the are destined to; most succeed because they are determined to.
Anatole France

To follow, without halt, one aim: there's the secret of success.
Anna Pavlova

The road to success is dotted with many tempting parking spaces.
Will Rogers

I was dressed for success. But success it never comes.
Stephen Malkmus

I couldn't wait for success so I went ahead without it.
Jonathan Winters

Success is not measured by what a man accomplishes, but by the opposition he has encountered, and the courage with which he maintained the struggle against overwhelming odds.
Charles A. Lindbergh

Success has always been easy to measure. It is the distance between one's origins and one's final achievement.
Michael Korda

There is no success without hardship.
Sophocles

The very essence of success is practice.
Ignace Paderewski

It takes 20 years to make an overnight success.
Eddie Cantor

Success usually comes to those who are too busy to be looking for it.
Henry David Thoreau

(To) know even one life has breathed easier because you have lived. This is to have succeeded.
Ralph Waldo Emerson

Symbolism

Sometimes a cigar is just a cigar.
Sigmund Freud

Symbols are just symbols; the thing's the thing.
Howard Ogden

There is no line between the "real world" and "world of myth and symbol". Objects, sensations, hit with the impact of hallucination.
William S. Burroughs

All art is at once surface and symbol. Those who go beneath the surface do so at their peril.
Oscar Wilde

Airplane, n. a sexual symbol useful for getting from Vienna to Berlin quickly.
The Surrealist Dictionary

A person gets from a symbol the meaning he puts into it, and what is one man's comfort and inspiration is another's jest and scorn.
Justice Robert Jackson

If you want a symbolic gesture don't burn the flag, wash it.
Norman Thomas

There is no surer way to misread any document than to read it literally.
Judge Learned Hand

The metaphor is perhaps one of man's most fruitful potentialities… and it seems a tool for creation which God forgot inside one of His creatures when He made him.
José Ortega y Gasset

Everything's a metaphor.
Johann Wolfgang von Goethe

Technology

The real danger is not that computers will begin to think like men, but that men will begin to think like computers.
Sydney J. Harris

Computers are useless. They can only give you answers.
Pablo Picasso

A computer is like an Old Testament god, with a lot of rules and no mercy.
Joseph Campbell

Never trust a computer you can't throw out a window.
Steve Wozniak

It is only when they go wrong that machines remind you how powerful they are.
Clive James

The more data banks record about each one of us, the less we exist.
Marshall McLuhan

Man is still the most extraordinary computer of all.
John F. Kennedy

The best computer is a man, and it's the only one that can be mass-produced by unskilled labor.
Wernher Von Braun

There are only two industries that refer to their customers as "users".
Edward Tufte

The street finds its own use for technology.
William Gibson

In this so-called age of technicians, the only battles we know how to fight are battles against windmills.
> Simone Weil

Technology is a way of organizing the universe so that man doesn't have to experience it.
> Max Frisch

The effort of using machines to mimic the human mind has always struck me as rather silly. I would rather use them to mimic something better.
> Edsger Dijkstra

One machine can do the work of fifty ordinary men. No machine can do the work of one extraordinary man.
> Elbert G. Hubbard

What scientists have in their briefcases is terrifying.
> Nikita Khrushchev

Technology... is a queer thing. It brings you great gifts with one hand, and it stabs you in the back with the other.
> C.P. Snow

The machine does not isolate man from the great problems of nature but plunges him more deeply into them.
> Antoine de Saint-Exupéry

It is a distinction between science and technology that technology must always be useful, whereas science need not be.
> Sir Patrick Linstead

Men have become the tools of their tools.
> Henry David Thoureau

If the human race wants to go to hell in a basket, technology can help it get there by jet.
> Charles M. Allen

A computer lets you make more mistakes faster than any invention in human history – with the possible exceptions of handguns and tequila.
> Mitch Ratcliffe

Technological progress has merely provided us with more efficient means for going backwards.
> Aldous Huxley

For a list of all the ways technology has failed to improve the quality of life, please press three.
> Alice Kahn

All technology should be assumed guilty until proven innocent.
> David Brower

It has become appallingly obvious that our technology has exceeded our humanity.
> Albert Einstein

Our scientific power has outrun our spiritual power. We have guided missiles and misguided men.
> Martin Luther King, Jr.

Technology makes it possible for people to gain control over everything, except over technology.
> John Tudor

Any sufficiently advanced technology is indistinguishable from magic.
> Arthur C. Clarke

Thought

Nurture your mind with great thoughts, for you will never go any higher than you think.
> Benjamin Disraeli

To achieve the impossible, it is precisely the unthinkable that must be thought.
> Tom Robbins

You are today where your thoughts have brought you; you will be tomorrow where your thoughts take you.
> James Allen

First thoughts have tremendous energy. It is the way the mind first flashes on something.
> Natalie Goldberg

First thought, best thought.
> Zen Saying

The mind is not a vessel to be filled but a fire to be kindled.
> Plutarch

What luck for rulers that men do not think.
> Adolf Hitler

Less than fifteen percent of the people do any original thinking on any subject. The greatest torture in the world for most people is to think.
> Luther Burbank

A great many people think they are thinking when they are merely rearranging their prejudices.
> William James

If you make people think they're thinking, they'll love you. But if you really make them think, they'll hate you.
> Don Marquis

There is nothing either good or bad but thinking makes it so.
> William Shakespeare

A mind is the most controlled substance there is.
> Steve Aylett

The mind embraces all the nobler aspirations but your body has all the fun.
> Woody Allen

Think for yourselves and let others enjoy the privilege to do so, too.
> Voltaire

The empires of the future are the empires of the mind.
> Winston Churchill

It is the mark of an educated mind to be able to entertain a thought without accepting it.
> Aristotle

We are what we think
All that we are arises
With our thoughts
With our thoughts
We make our world.
> Buddha

A man is what he thinks about all day long.
> Ralph Waldo Emerson

I think; therefore I am.
> René Descartes

If little else, the brain is an educational toy.
> Tom Robbins

What was once thought can never be unthought.
   Friedrich Dürrenmatt

Nothing divides one so much as thought.
   Reginald Blyth

There are no dangerous thoughts; thinking itself is dangerous.
   Hannah Arendt

Beware when the great God lets loose a thinker on this planet.
   Ralph Waldo Emerson

Thought is action in rehearsal.
   Sigmund Freud

Think before you think!
   Stanislaw J. Lec

Brain: an apparatus with which we think we think.
   Ambrose Bierce

A conclusion is simply the place where someone got tired of thinking.
   Arthur Block

I spent most of my time thinking, because I didn't have enough energy to do
anything else.
   Banana Yoshimoto

The only reason some people get lost in thought is because it is unfamiliar territory.
   Paul Fix

His mind wanders but it never gets very far.
   Archie, describing Jughead

I can't understand it. I can't even understand the people who can understand it.
   Queen Juliana of the Netherlands

Anyone who isn't confused really doesn't understand the situation.
   Edward R. Murrow

If I look confused it's because I'm thinking.
   Samuel Goldwyn

The doctors X-rayed my head and found nothing.
   Dizzy Dean, after being hit on the head by a ball in the 1934 World Series

Time

Time is a storm in which we are all lost.
    William Carlos Williams

There is never enough time, unless you're serving it.
    Malcolm Forbes

Tempus fugit (time flies)
    Ovid

Time flies and time crawls. Like an insect up and down the walls.
    Howard Devoto

The bad news is time flies. The good news is you're the pilot.
    Michael Althsuler

Time sneaks up on you like a windshield on a bug.
    John Lithgow

Time is the most valuable thing a man can spend.
    Theophrastus

You can't waste time and you can't save time; you can only choose what you do at any given moment.
    James Gleick

At my back I always hear time's winged chariot hurrying near.
    Andrew Marvell

You may delay, but time will not.
    Benjamin Franklin

Time and tide wait for no man.
    Geoffrey Chaucer

Remember that lost time does not return.
Thomas á Kempis

I wasted time, and now doth time waste me.
    William Shakespeare

The time you enjoy wasting is not wasted time.
    Bertrand Russell

Time is the reef upon which all our frail mystic ships are wrecked.
    Noel Coward

Time is the moving image of reality.
        Plato

Time is not a line, but a series of now-points.
        Taisen Deshimaru

You mean now?
        Yogi Berra, when asked for the time of day

Let your life lightly dance on the edges of Time like dew on the tip of a leaf.
        Rabindranath Tagore

Time is dead as long as it is being clicked off by little wheels; only when the
clock stops does time come to life.
        William Faulkner

We didn't lose the game; we just ran out of time.
        Vince Lombardi

Time is a river which carries me along, but I am the river; it is a tiger that
devours me, but I am the tiger.
        Jorge Luis Borges

Time is but the stream I go a-fishing in.
        Henry David Thoreau

Time is the fire in which we burn.
        Gene Roddenberry

Time is that in which all things pass away.
        Arthur Schopenhauer

Since time is the one immaterial object which we cannot influence – neither speed up
nor slow down, add to nor diminish – it is an imponderably valuable gift.
        Maya Angelou

I recommend to you to take care of the minutes; for hours will take care
of themselves.
        Lord Chesterfield

Dost thou love life, then do not squander time, for that's the stuff life is made of.
        Benjamin Franklin

As if you could kill time without injuring eternity.
        Henry David Thoreau

All my possessions for a moment of time.
        Queen Elizabeth I, last words

What do I want? I want yesterday.
Natalie Wood

Time is what we want most, but... what we use worst.
William Penn

We must use time as a tool, not as a crutch.
John F. Kennedy

Who forces time is pushed back by time; who yields to time finds time on his side.
The Talmud

Time is the wisest counselor of all.
Pericles

Time is the fairest and toughest judge.
Edgar Quinet

Time is a great teacher, but unfortunately it kills all its pupils.
Louis-Hector Berlioz

Time wounds all heels.
Jane Sherwood Ace

Tobacco, coffee, alcohol, hashish, prussic acid, strychnine, are weak dilutions; the surest poison is time.
Ralph Waldo Emerson

For tribal man space was the uncontrollable mystery. For technological man it is time that occupies the same role.
Marshall McLuhan

Time is not measured by the passing of years, but by what one does, what one feels and what one achieves.
Jawaharlal Nehru

To realize the unimportance of time is the gate of wisdom.
Bertrand Russell

Time is what prevents everything from happening at once.
John Archibald Wheeler

Trust

Trust everybody, but cut the cards.
  Finley Peter Dunne

Trust in Allah, but tie your camel.
  Arabian Proverb

A man who doesn't trust himself can never really trust anyone else.
  Cardinal de Retz

As soon as you trust yourself, you will know how to live.
  Johann Wolfgang von Goethe

Trust thyself: every heart vibrates to that iron string.
  Ralph Waldo Emerson

When I'm trusting and being myself as fully as possible, everything in my life
reflects this by falling into place easily, often miraculously.
  Shakti Gawain

Do not trust all men, but trust men of worth; the former course is silly,
the latter a mark of prudence.
  Democritus

It is an equal failing to trust everybody, and to trust nobody.
  English Proverb

Love all, trust a few.
  William Shakespeare

Never trust the man who tells you all his troubles but keeps from you all his joys.
  Jewish Proverb

Never trust a man who speaks well of everybody.
  John Churton Collins

Never trust anyone over 30.
  1960's generation slogan

Never trust a fucking hippie.
  John Lydon, a.k.a. Johnny Rotten

Learning to trust is one of life's most difficult tasks.
  Isaac Watts

It is more shameful to distrust one's friends than to be deceived by them.
  François duc de la Rochefoucauld

You may be deceived if you trust too much, but you will live in torment if you don't trust enough.
    Frank Crane

No man ever quite believes in any other man. One may believe in an idea absolutely, but not in a man.
    H.L. Mencken

To be trusted is a greater compliment than to be loved.
    George MacDonald

Put more trust in nobility of character than in an oath.
    Solon

Truth

Truth is always paradoxical.
    Henry David Thoreau

Truth is what most contradicts itself.
    Lawrence Durrell

Truth is never pure, and rarely simple.
    Oscar Wilde

I want to know the truth, however perverted that may sound.
    Stephen Wolfram

All great truths begin as blasphemies.
    George Bernard Shaw

When we discover that the truth is already in us, we are all at once our original selves.
    Dogen Zenji

To thine own self be true, and it must follow, as the night the day, thou canst not then be false to any man.
    William Shakespeare

Truth and oil always come to the surface.
    Spanish Proverb

The truth dazzles gradually, or else the world would be blind.
    Emily Dickinson

The best mind-altering drug is truth.
        Lily Tomlin

Truth is eternal, knowledge is changeable. It is disastrous to confuse them.
        Madeleine L'Engle

There's a little truth in all jive, and a little jive in all truth.
        Leonard Barnes

When you want to fool the world, tell the truth.
        Otto Von Bismarck

Truth has a handsome countenance but torn garments.
        German Proverb

Truth looks tawdry when she is overdressed.
        Rabindranath Tagore

Truth exists, only falsehood has to be invented.
        Georges Braque

Truth is beautiful, without doubt; but so are lies.
        Ralph Waldo Emerson

The truth isn't beautiful, but the hunger for it is.
        Nadine Gordimer

It is always the best policy to speak the truth. Unless of course, you are
an exceptionally good liar.
        Jerome K. Jerome

Get the facts first. You can distort them later.
        Mark Twain

Say not, "I have found the truth," but rather, "I have found a truth."
        Kahlil Gibran

Respect for the truth comes close to being the basis for all morality.
        Frank Herbert

All great truths are simple in final analysis, and easily understood; if they are not,
they are not great truths.
        Napoleon Hill

The great seal of truth is simplicity.
        Herman Boerhaave

All truths are easy to understand once they are discovered; the point is to discover them.
>Galileo Galilei

The terrible thing about the quest for truth is that you find it.
>Rémy de Gourmont

Truth may walk through the world unarmed.
>Bedouin Proverb

Everything you add to the truth subtracts from the truth.
>Alexander Solzhenitsyn

The truth is always the strongest argument.
>Sophocles

In a minority of one, the truth is still the truth
>Mahatma Gandhi

The truth is incontrovertible. Malice may attack it, ignorance may deride it, but in the end, there it is.
>Winston Churchill

Whatever separates you from the Truth, throw it away, it will vanish anyhow.
>Yumus Emre

Just get rid of the false and you will automatically realize the true.
>Ho-shan

We arrive at truth, not by reason only, but also by the heart.
>Blaise Pascal

I don't want yes men around me. I want everyone to tell the truth, even if it costs them their jobs.
>Samuel Goldwyn

I never gave anyone hell. I just told the truth and they thought it was hell.
>Harry Truman

The truth does not change according to our ability to stomach it.
>Flannery O'Connor

Tell the truth and run.
>Yugoslavian Proverb

In time of war the first casualty is truth.
>Boake Carter

If you have a gun, you can shoot one, two, three, five people; but if you have an ideology that you think is the absolute truth, you can kill millions.
> Thich Nhat Hanh

I would give my life for a man who is looking for the truth. But I would gladly kill a man who thinks he has found it.
> Luis Buñuel

Between truth and the search for it, I choose the second.
> Bernard Berenson

The pursuit of truth will set you free; even if you never catch up with it.
> Clarence Darrow

A man that seeks truth and loves it must be reckoned precious to any human society.
> Epictetus

The search for truth is more precious than its possession.
> Albert Einstein

My way of joking is to tell the truth. It's the funniest joke in the world.
> George Bernard Shaw

All truth passes through three stages. First, it is ridiculed. Second, it is violently opposed. Third, it is accepted as being self-evident.
> Arthur Schopenhauer

Truth is not feasible, mankind doesn't deserve it.
> Sigmund Freud

As scarce as truth is, the supply has always been in excess of the demand.
> Josh Billings

Never assume the obvious is true.
> William Safire

The obscure we see eventually. The completely obvious, it seems, takes longer.
> Edward R. Murrow

One always has the air of someone who is lying when one speaks to a policeman.
> Charles-Louis Philippe

It is hard to believe that a man is telling the truth when you know that you would lie if you were in his place.
> H.L. Mencken

I prefer to be true to myself, even at the hazard of incurring the ridicule of others, rather than to be false, and to incur my own abhorrence.
Frederick Douglass

I must find a truth that is true for me.
Søren Kierkegaard

In the province of the mind, what one believes to be true either is true, or becomes true.
John C. Lilly

But it is not enough to possess a truth; it is essential that the truth should possess us.
Maurice Maeterlinck

There are no facts, only interpretations.
Friedrich Nietzsche

The first rule is to keep an untroubled spirit. The second is to look things in the face and know them for what they are.
Marcus Aurelius

Men occasionally stumble over the truth, but most of them pick themselves up and hurry off as if nothing ever happened.
Winston Churchill

To know, to get into the truth of anything, is ever a mystic act, of which the best logics can but babble on the surface.
Thomas Carlyle

Truth is the safest lie.
Yiddish Proverb

A liar needs a good memory.
Marcus Fabius Quintalianus

That's not a lie, it's a terminological inexactitude.
Alexander Haig

Of all the animals, man is the only one that lies.
Mark Twain

A lie gets halfway around the world before the truth has a chance to get its pants on.
Winston Churchill

A lie told often enough becomes truth.
Vladimir Ilich Lenin

Never admit a lie. Just keep repeating it.
Joseph Goebbels

Anyone who tells the truth is bound to be found out, sooner or later.
Oscar Wilde

Truth conquers all things.
Latin Proverb

Truth can be a dangerous thing. It is quite patient and relentless.
R. Scott Richards

Rather than love, than money, than fame, give me truth.
Henry David Thoreau

Truth is more of a stranger than fiction.
Mark Twain

Ye shall know the truth, and the truth shall make you free.
Bible, John 8:32

Vice

It has been my experience that folks who have no vices have very few virtues.
Abraham Lincoln

He has all the virtues I dislike and none of the vices I admire.
Winston Churchill

I have not a particle of confidence in a man who has no redeeming vices.
Mark Twain

Every vice is only an exaggeration of a necessary and virtuous function.
Ralph Waldo Emerson

It is good to be without vices, but it is not good to be without temptations.
Walter Bagehot

The vices we scoff at in others laugh at us within ourselves.
Sir Thomas Browne

The virtue of some people consists wholly in condemning the vices in others.
Herbert Samuel

It is the function of vice to keep virtue within reasonable bounds.
Samuel Butler

Men are more easily governed by their vices than through their virtues.
    Napoleon Bonaparte

Our faith comes in moments; our vice is habitual.
    William Ellery Channing

Vice knows she's ugly, so puts on her mask.
    Benjamin Franklin

Wild oats make a bad autumn crop.
    Cynic's Calendar

Vices are their own punishment.
    Aesop

Vice is its own reward.
    Quentin Crisp

Every vice has its excuse ready.
    Publilius Syrus

What were once vices are the fashion of the day.
    Seneca

When choosing between two evils, I always like to try the one I've never tried before.
    Mae West

There's a million ways of licking honey off of razors.
    Stuart Davis

Here's a rule I recommend. Never practice two vices at once.
    Tallulah Bankhead

Vision

Vision is the art of seeing things invisible.
    Jonathan Swift

A rock pile ceases to be a rock pile the moment a single man contemplates it, bearing within him the image of a cathedral.
    Antoine de Saint-Exupéry

I shut my eyes in order to see.
    Paul Gauguin

I skate to where the puck is going to be, not where it has been.
Wayne Gretzky

Vision looks inwards and becomes duty. Vision looks outwards and becomes aspiration. Vision looks upwards and becomes faith.
Stephen S. Wise

I can see… in what you call the dark, but which to me is golden. I can see a God-made world, not a manmade world.
Helen Keller

Every man takes the limits of his own field of vision for the limits of the world.
Arthur Schopenhauer

People only see what they are prepared to see.
Ralph Waldo Emerson

We don't see things as they are, we see them as we are.
Anaïs Nin

Our limited perspective, our hopes and fears become our measure of life, and when circumstances don't fit our ideas, they become our difficulties.
Benjamin Franklin

When it is darkest, men see the stars.
Ralph Waldo Emerson

Visionary people are visionary partly because of the very great things they don't see.
Berkeley Rice

The most pathetic person in the world is someone who has sight but has no vision.
Helen Keller

Just because a man lacks the use of his eyes doesn't mean he lacks vision.
Stevie Wonder

In the country of the blind the one-eyed man is king.
Michael Apostolius

It's not what you look at that matters, it's what you see.
Henry David Thoreau

One sees great things from the valley, only small things from the peak.
G.K. Chesterton

No man sees far; the most see not farther than their noses.
Thomas Carlyle

Where there is no vision the people perish...
Bible, Proverbs 29:18

The only limits are, as always, those of vision.
James Broughton

You don't need a weatherman to know which way the wind blows.
Bob Dylan

Your vision will become clear only when you can look into your own heart.
Who looks outside, dreams; who looks inside, awakes.
Carl Jung

Vision without action is merely a dream. Action without vision just passes the time.
Vision with action can change the world.
Joel Barker

Will

Mind moves matter.
Virgil

Strength does not come from physical capacity. It comes from an indomitable will.
Mahatma Gandhi

People do not lack strength; they lack will.
Victor Hugo

If we cannot do what we will, we must will what we can.
Yiddish Proverb

The will is never free – it is always attached or an object, a purpose. It is simply
the engine in the car – it can't steer.
Joyce Cary

Will springs from the two elements of moral sense and self-interest.
Abraham Lincoln

Life is like a game of cards. The hand that is dealt you represents determinism;
the way you play it is free will.
Jawaharlal Nehru

Be there a will, and wisdom finds a way.
George Crabbe

Where there's a will, there's a way.
English Proverb

When the will is ready the feet are light.
Proverb

We do not walk on our legs, but on our will.
Sufi Proverb

Great souls have wills; feeble ones have only wishes.
Chinese Proverb

Will is character in action.
William McDougall

He who can follow his own will is a king.
Irish Proverb

Love God and do what you will.
Saint Augustine

Wisdom

Be wiser than other people if you can; but do not tell them so.
Lord Chesterfield

It is not wise to be wiser than necessary.
Philippe Quinault

The art of being wise is the art of knowing what to overlook.
William James

A wise man never knows all, only fools know everything.
African Proverb

The fool doth think he is wise, but the wise man knows himself to be a fool.
William Shakespeare

A wise man may look ridiculous in the company of fools.
English proverb

Wisdom is the principal thing, therefore get wisdom; and with all thy getting, get understanding.
Bible, Proverbs, 4:7

The invariable mark of wisdom is to see the miraculous in the common.
Ralph Waldo Emerson

Wisdom begins in wonder.
Socrates

Wisdom begins at the end.
Daniel Webster

Wisdom cries out in the streets, and no man regards it.
William Shakespeare

Wisdom is not acquired save as the result of investigation.
Sankara Acharya

We don't receive wisdom; we must discover it for ourselves after a journey that no one can take for us or spare us.
Marcel Proust

Knowledge is a process of piling up facts; wisdom lies in their simplification.
Martin H. Fischer

Knowledge speaks, but wisdom listens.
Jimi Hendrix

To acquire knowledge, one must study; but to acquire wisdom, one must observe.
Marilyn Vos Savant

One's first step in wisdom is to question everything – and one's last is to come to terms with everything.
Georg Christoph Lichtenberg

Wisdom is the power to put our time and our knowledge to the proper use.
Thomas J. Watson

If I ever acquire wisdom I suppose I shall be wise enough to know what to do with it.
W. Somerset Maugham

For wisdom is better than jewels, and all that you may desire cannot compare with her.
Bible, Proverbs 8:11

The doors of wisdom are never shut.
Benjamin Franklin

True wisdom lies in gathering the precious things out of each day as it goes by.
E.S. Bouton

Time ripens all things; no man is born wise.
> Miguel de Cervantes

Young men are apt to think themselves wise enough, as drunken men are apt to think themselves sober enough.
> Lord Chesterfield

The price of wisdom is above rubies.
> Bible, Job 28:18

There is a wisdom of the head, and a wisdom of the heart.
> Charles Dickens

Pain makes man think. Thought makes man wise. Wisdom makes life endurable.
> John Patrick

It is more easy to be wise for others than for ourselves.
> François duc de la Rochefoucauld

Do not seek to follow in the footsteps of the wise. Seek what they sought.
> Basho

Women

Women who seek to be equal with men lack ambition.
> Timothy Leary

When a woman behaves like a man why doesn't she behave like a nice man?
> Dame Edith Evans

Well-behaved women rarely make history.
> Laurel Thatcher Ulrich

Of all the wild beasts of land or sea, the wildest is woman.
> Menander

The female of the species is more deadly than the male.
> Rudyard Kipling

Woman was God's second mistake.
> Friedrich Nietzsche

Women are really much nicer than men. No wonder we like them.
> Kingsley Amis

Women are wiser than men because they know less and understand more.
James Thurber

With women, the heart argues, not the mind.
Matthew Arnold

Women are like dreams – they are never the way you would like to have them.
Luigi Pirandello

I married beneath me. All women do.
Lady Astor

Being a woman is a terrible trade, since it consists principally of dealing with men.
Joseph Conrad

If men knew how women pass the time when they are alone, they'd never marry.
O. Henry

Ah, women. They make the highs higher and the lows more frequent.
Friedrich Nietzsche

Behind every successful man is a surprised woman.
Maryon Pearson

Women are like elephants to me. I like to look at 'em, but I wouldn't want to own one.
W.C. Fields

Women and elephants never forget an injury.
H.H. Munro, a.k.a. Saki

The entire being of a woman is a secret which should be kept.
Isak Dinesen

Women should be obscene and not heard.
Groucho Marx

Women in general want to be loved for what they are and men for what they accomplish.
Theodor Reik

The whole thing about the women is, the lust to be misunderstood.
Will Rogers

Any woman who has a great deal to offer the world is in trouble.
Hazel Scott

Woman is the Nigger of the World.
        John Lennon & Yoko Ono

A woman without a man is like a fish without a bicycle.
        Gloria Steinem

Wonder

Wonder is the beginning of wisdom.
        Greek Proverb

Wonder, rather than doubt, is the root of knowledge.
        Abraham Heschel

Philosophy begins in wonder. And, at the end, when philosophic thought has done
its best, the wonder remains.
        Alfred North Whitehead

From wonder into wonder existence opens.
        Lao-Tzu

Wonder is the basis of worship.
        Thomas Carlyle

It was through the feeling of wonder that men now and at first began to philosophize.
        Aristotle

The world will never starve for want of wonders.
        G.K. Chesterson

Awe is what moves us forward.
        Joseph Campbell

He who can no longer pause to wonder and stand rapt in awe, is as good as dead;
his eyes are closed.
        Albert Einstein

Look at everything as though you were seeing it either for the first or last time.
        Betty Smith

We carry with us the wonders we seek without us.
        Sir Thomas Browne

It is not ignorance but knowledge which is the mother of wonder.
        Joseph Wood Krutch

Man does not seem to be endowed with an infinite capacity for wonder.
    Louis Aragon

Explanation separates us from astonishment, which is the only gateway to the incomprehensible.
    Eugène Ionesco

Sell your cleverness and buy bewilderment.
    Mevlâna Jalâladdîn Rumi

Be on your guard against too much cleverness.
    Hermann Hesse

To be matter of fact about the world is to blunder into fantasy – and dull fantasy at that – as the real world is strange and wonderful.
    Robert A. Heinlein

He who wonders discovers that this in itself is wonder.
    M.C. Escher

I've had a perfectly wonderful evening. But this wasn't it.
    Groucho Marx

Work

Put your talent into your work, but your genius into your life.
    Oscar Wilde

A man's life is his work; his work is his life.
    Jackson Pollack

Fundamentally, we work to create, and only incidentally do we work to eat.
    Willis Harman

Work to become, not to acquire.
    Elbert G. Hubbard

It is your work in life that is the ultimate seduction.
    Pablo Picasso

Only work which is the product of inner compulsion can have spiritual meaning.
    Walter Groupius

The highest reward for a person's toil is not what they get from it, but what they become by it.
    John Ruskin

That's what we're all looking for, the place where the work leads us.
    Dustin Hoffman

All true work is religion.
    Thomas Carlyle

It is the quality of our work which will please God and not the quantity.
    Mahatma Gandhi

The days you work are the best days.
    Georgia O'Keefe

Ya gots to work with what you gots to work with.
    Stevie Wonder

The biggest mistake we could ever make in our lives is to think we work for anybody but ourselves.
    Brian Tracy

The work praises the man.
    Irish Proverb

The work will teach you how to do it.
    Estonian Proverb

When your work speaks for itself, don't interrupt.
    Henry John Kaiser

You must judge a man by the work of his hands.
    African Proverb

Ye shall know them by their works.
    Bible, Matthew 7:20

It is a commonplace observation that work expands so as to fill the time available for its completion.
    C. Northcote Parkinson

My work is done. Why wait?
    George Eastman, suicide note

There is no substitute for hard work.
    Thomas Edison

Hard work never killed anybody, but why take a chance?
    B. Bergen

I find that the harder I work, the more luck I seem to have.
Thomas Jefferson

The harder you work, the harder it is to surrender.
Vince Lombardi

I like work: it fascinates me. I can sit and look at it for hours.
Jerome K. Jerome

It takes little effort to watch a man carry a load.
Chinese Proverb

The world is filled with willing people; some willing to work, the rest willing to let them.
Robert Frost

I am a friend of the workingman, I would rather be his friend than be one.
Clarence Darrow

People who work sitting down get paid more than people who work standing up.
Odgen Nash

Distrust any enterprise that requires new clothes.
Henry David Thoreau

Work is a necessary evil to be avoided.
Mark Twain

One of the symptoms of an approaching nervous breakdown is the belief that one's work is terribly important.
Bertrand Russell

I worked myself up from nothing to a state of extreme poverty.
Groucho Marx

Work is the curse of the drinking classes.
Mike Romanoff

When a man tells you that he got rich through hard work, ask him: "whose?"
Don Marquis

Work is the only dirty four-letter word in the language.
Abbie Hoffman

Work is the province of cattle.
Dorothy Parker

It's only work if somebody makes you do it.
> Bill Watterson

He who considers his work beneath him will be above doing it well.
> Alexander Chase

Without work all life goes rotten.
> Albert Camus

Work spares us from three great evils: boredom, vice and need.
> Voltaire

Blessed is he who has found his work. Let him ask no other blessedness.
> Thomas Carlyle

Far and away the best prize that life offers is the chance to work hard at work worth doing.
> Theodore Roosevelt

Unless your work gives you trouble, it is no good.
> Pablo Picasso

My work is a game, a very serious game.
> M.C. Escher

Basically, I no longer work for anything but the sensation I have while working.
> Albert Giacometti, sculptor

The supreme accomplishment is to blur the line between work and play.
> Arnold Toynbee

Work and play are words used to describe the same thing under differing conditions.
> Mark Twain

Zen

Be quite still and solitary. The world will freely offer itself to you.
> Franz Kafka

No one can see their reflection in running water. It is only in still water that we can see.
> Taoist Proverb

Thinking is what gets you caught from behind.
> O.J. Simpson

God made everything out of nothing, but the nothingness shows through.
Paul Valéry

What happens to the hole when the cheese is gone?
Bertolt Brecht, Western Koan

Knock on the sky and listen to the sound.
Zen Saying

'Scuse me while I kiss the sky.
Jimi Hendrix

The only zen you find on the tops of mountains is the zen you bring up there.
Robert M. Pirsig

When you seek it, you cannot find it.
Zen Koan

You don't look for something, it's sure to be found.
Mick Jones

Fundamentally, the marksman aims at himself.
Eugen Herrigel

The miracle is not to fly in the air, or to walk on the water, but to walk on the earth.
Chinese Proverb

The true way goes over a rope which is not stretched at any great height... It seems more designed to make men stumble, than to be walked upon.
Franz Kafka

In walking, just walk. In sitting, just sit. Above all, don't wobble.
Yun-Men

Seize from every moment its unique novelty and do not prepare your joys
Andre Gide

I do not cut my life up into days but my days into lives, each day, each hour, an entire life.
Juan Ramón Jiménez

Just this!
Zen Saying

Zen teaches nothing; it merely enables us to wake up and become aware.
It does not teach, it points.
D.T. Suzuki

Zen is a finger pointing at the moon.
Zen Proverb

When you do something, you should burn yourself completely, like a good bonfire, leaving no trace of yourself.
Shunryu Suzuki Roshi

Cease from practice based on intellectual understanding, pursuing words, and following after speech, and learn the backward step that turns your light inward to illuminate your self.
Dogen Zenji

Go into yourself and see how deep the place is from which your life flows.
Rainer Maria Rilke

Index